SCIENTIFIC WRITING FOR

GRADUATE STUDENTS

Committee on Graduate Training in Scientific Writing
Ellsworth B. Cook
Edwin L. Cooper
James Forbes
Theodore Melnechuk
Marcus Rosenblum
F. Peter Woodford

Other books published by the Council of Biology Editors, Inc.
CBE Style Manual, 5th edition, 1983
Economics of Scientific Journals, 1982

SCIENTIFIC WRITING FOR GRADUATE STUDENTS

A Manual on the Teaching of Scientific Writing

Prepared by
COMMITTEE ON GRADUATE TRAINING
IN SCIENTIFIC WRITING

Edited by
F. PETER WOODFORD

Published by
COUNCIL OF BIOLOGY EDITORS, INC.
Bethesda, Maryland

Library of Congress Cataloging-in-Publication Data
Main entry under title:

Scientific writing for graduate students.

Bibliography: p.
Includes indexes.
1. Technical writing.   I. Woodford, F. Peter,
1930–   II. Council of Biology Editors.   Committee
on Graduate Training in Scientific Writing.
T11.S39   1986   808'.0666021   85-29945
ISBN 0-914340-06-9 (pbk.)

First edition 1968

First reprinting 1976

Second reprinting 1981

Third reprinting 1983

Fourth reprinting, with references updated by F. Peter Woodford, 1986

PREFACE

For the teachers of scientific writing
to whom this manual is addressed

This book has been written because the members of the Council of Biology Editors, like all editors of scientific journals, are acutely aware that many scientists write badly. It is no longer the exception but the rule that scientific writing is heavy, verbose, pretentious, and dull. Considering that the scientists who produce it have received advanced university training, this is little less than shocking. We asked ourselves why these highly educated and intelligent men and women should express themselves so obscurely, so wordily, and therefore so ineffectually. Although the reasons may be complex, one contributing factor seems clear: few universities provide formal training in scientific writing, and few even encourage their students to develop a rational technique for writing scientific papers through the study of any of the excellent available textbooks.

We believe that this hiatus in university curricula should be remedied, and that formal instruction in scientific writing should form an integral part of a scientist's university training. Although for successful scientific writing a sound knowledge of English grammar and composition is necessary, it is not sufficient. The considerations involved in this kind of writing are too profound and too subtle to be satisfactorily dealt with at an elementary level, either in high school or in college. They necessitate hard thinking about the requirements of scientific proof, the logical development of scientific argument, and precision of scientific expression. For these reasons we believe that the instruction is most effectively given at a late stage of a scientist's training—in graduate school—and that it is best given by a scientist. A graduate student is also more interested than an undergraduate in learning how to write scientific prose, because not only his dissertation, but his first journal articles are in the offing. He is more easily inspired to learn from someone who is, like him, deeply concerned with scientific research than from one who is only peripherally involved.

For the most part, then, we envisage that the teaching of scientific writing will be undertaken by scientists who are on university faculties and who are already much occupied with other duties. We have tried to save their time by collecting in one volume the widely scattered source materials and references necessary for the preparation of a course and by providing a framework of instruction from which they can work with the minimum of preparation. Naturally, we recognize that the method of teaching advocated here is only one of many possibilities, and that any teacher worth his salt develops his own techniques, chooses his own timing, and injects his own humor and personality into his course. We hope that the brevity of our text will show that we have tried to leave room for such individual treatment and that we do not intend the course to be followed rigidly and unimaginatively.

The timing given at the beginning of most of the chapters is based on actual experience in one-hour seminar sessions with about 20 students. Of course, instructors with differently timed sessions under different circumstances can make their own interpretation of these indications. The steps in writing a journal article have been grouped into chapters (numbered 2–9) according to a logical scheme, but there is no need for the end of a session to coincide with the end of a chapter. On the contrary, sessions can be broken off at the conclusion of any of the small steps listed and described.

From the foregoing it is clear that the manual is intended primarily for use by the *teacher* of scientific writing, and is therefore different in purpose from the many textbooks of scientific writing that are meant to be used by the student himself. Nevertheless, sufficiently motivated students will be able to use this manual directly if no instructor is available.

Because we are editors of biological and biochemical journals, we have confined our attention to the characteristics, the faults, and the subject matter of the kind of writing we encounter in the literature of the life sciences. It is probable, however, that the principles here set down apply to other scientific disciplines as well, and we expect that this book will be usable, with appropriate modifications, by scientists in other fields. In our opinion, much of the nonscientific literature that comes our way is also pompous and longwinded, and perhaps some of our strictures on faults of style might be taken to heart by nonscientists, too; but we do not wish to press the point.

Perhaps a word of explanation about the arrangement of the book is necessary. A "basic" course in scientific writing is contained in Chapters 1–10; this can be given in about 12 one-hour sessions. Chapters 11–14 contain material on other topics in scientific communication and can be incorporated or added at the instructor's discretion. Although all members of the Committee have read and criticized all drafts of each chapter and endorse the final form they have taken, we have decided to indicate who has written each chapter because we each want to take responsibility for any faults the chapter may contain and to stress that some of the contents are inevitably matters of personal opinion. In particular, we emphasize that the stand we have taken about doctoral dissertations (Chapter 11) may be in conflict with the current policy of many universities. For the markedly different styles employed by the different authors we make no apology; even though we all subscribe to the same principles of scientific writing, we strongly believe that such writing need not be uniform or colorless, and we expect each author's personality to be discernible through what he writes.

We are aware that this manual is only a start, a single step in what we believe to be the right direction: the introduction of courses of instruction in scientific writing into university graduate schools. We are sure that the book has shortcomings, but we must rely on wider experience in its application to set them right. We welcome all criticisms and suggestions from its readers that will increase the usefulness of the manual in future editions. Even if the present manual falls far short of being the perfect guide for instructors, we shall feel that its major objective will have been attained if its publication makes the academic community aware that the teaching of scientific writing is an essential element in the training of every scientist.

Council of Biology Editors' Committee on Graduate
Training in Scientific Writing

Ellsworth B. Cook	Theodore Melnechuk
Edwin L. Cooper	Marcus Rosenblum
James Forbes	F. Peter Woodford

CONTENTS

ACKNOWLEDGMENTS

It is a great pleasure to acknowledge help given to the Committee by the following individuals, by virtue both of their rigorous criticism and their generous encouragement: Warren Weaver, vice-president of the Sloan Foundation and scientific communicator par excellence; John T. Edsall, ex-editor of the Journal of Biological Chemistry and professor of biochemistry at Harvard University; William A. Bayless, director of The Rockefeller University Press; Margaret Mahoney of the Carnegie Corporation, New York; Lois DeBakey, professor of scientific communication at Tulane University; E. H. Ahrens, Jr. and Bruce A. Barron, of The Rockefeller University; Dorald A. Allred of Brigham Young University; P. W. Wilson of the University of Wisconsin; and many others. The Committee was set up under the wise direction of Robert E. Gordon and has been guided throughout by his seasoned advice. Finally, we are indebted to the preliminary work of the previous CBE Committee on Graduate Training in Scientific Writing under the chairmanship of David E. Davis.

With the generous financial support of the Alfred P. Sloan Foundation, the Council of Biology Editors was able to organize a series of annual workshops, beginning in 1967, on the teaching of scientific writing and to introduce an early draft of this manual to those who were to be the pioneers in its use. We are deeply grateful for the constructive criticism we received from all the workshop participants, and particularly from L. W. Billingsley, William R. Lockhart, Robert W. Pennak, E. S. Nasset, and Juanita H. Williams.

WRITING A JOURNAL ARTICLE

WRITING A JOURNAL ARTICLE

1

Clearing Away the Underbrush

Timing:

Allow about 15 minutes for this introductory material, and plan to go well into Chapter 2 during your first session.

Most of the students who have signed up for your course will have done so because they are afraid of and dislike writing: they have no instinctive feeling for the power and beauty of words and no gift for putting them together tellingly. They like science because it is full of experimental action and definite, verifiable facts; writing, on the contrary, seems to be a less exciting activity requiring intuition, for which they have small use, and taste, for which they have no use at all.

Your first job is to convince them that *scientific* writing is an activity they will enjoy. It demands exactly the same qualities of thought as are needed for the rest of science: logic, clarity, and precision. A sense of literary "rightness" is definitely not necessary (although the few who have such a sense should not feel disadvantaged). Assure your students that if they will only apply scientific principles to the planning, design, and execution of scientific writing, they will surely master it. For scientific principles are, in essence, merely guidelines for keeping thought logical, clear, and precise; and the outstanding characteristics of successful scientific writing are that it is logically constructed, clearly expressed, and precisely worded.

Your students will have spent most of their university careers studying scientific principles, and their minds have been developed, therefore, in just the direction needed for good scientific writing. Urge them to get rid of the notion that because they are scientists they must of necessity be inferior writers. Quite the reverse is true, at least for the kind of writing with which this book is concerned. At its best, such writing is straightforward, concrete, exact, rigorous, clearheaded, and concise. Are not these the qualities most of us associate with scientists? Are they not the qualities your students are proud to possess to a highly developed degree?

Tell them how lucky they are. Both training and inclination predispose them to succeed in scientific writing, which is the only kind they need produce. Conversely, the "literary style" they dread, and for which they are neither suited nor trained, is not called for in scientific writing. In earlier courses in English composition they may have come to loathe all considerations of imponderable taste and nuance, to detest all subtle questions of balance and rhythm, and to distrust from the bottom of their hearts the phrasemaker and all his works. Emphasize that you are not qualified to teach literary style, and that they have not been assembled to learn it. For the task in hand—scientific writing—they need only be honestly, completely, and thoroughly scientific.

Do not be tempted, however, to go a step further and rhapsodize about how easy scientific writing is. It is not. To keep to a straight and narrow path through a thicket of complex and intertwining ideas can be extremely difficult. But it is no *more* difficult than keeping a line of research straight in the face of obstructive practical difficulties and tempting byways of investigation. And it is equally important.

If your students have been recruited not by the force of attraction (the desire to write well) but by that of compulsion (the desire of others that they write well), some may be less interested in whether they *can* improve their writing than in why they *should*. Tell such students that if they go into research—academic or industrial—they will, as a matter of course, be obliged to write papers for publication, and if they express themselves badly their papers will not be accepted in reputable journals. If they do succeed in publishing—in journals with lower standards—papers that are difficult to understand or that do not present arguments and results convincingly, their work will be disregarded and their scientific abilities will go unnoticed. Most established scientists, tolerant as they are of some faults of writing, recognize that consistently poor writing either betrays the inability to think clearly or reveals an unwillingness to take the trouble to do so. If the budding scientist wants to do himself justice, therefore, he simply must learn to write as well as he thinks.

Having made these points, ask your class to name the various kinds of writing that a scientist is called upon to produce. These include a dissertation at the start of his career; progress reports and survey papers for his close colleagues; case histories, if he is a medical man; journal articles for an audience of specialists; review articles for the less specialized; book reviews to be savored by the cognoscenti; project proposals and grant applications to be judged both by his peers and by laymen; and articles for a nonscientific but informed public. He will also have to write when he prepares talks for various types of audience. Stress that the good writer is like a well-mannered man: he is considerate of others. He must know who his readers or listeners are and aim, with this knowledge in mind, for the most rapid and comfortable communication possible.

Remind your students that writing is not extrinsic to research: it is inevitably a part of it, since research is not complete until it is published. At the same time you should, perhaps, reassure them by saying that although the first paper is notoriously the most difficult, you hope to take the sting out of even that most traumatic experience.

In this manual we suggest that you teach scientific writing not by enunciating abstract principles but, more concretely, by showing your class how to write a journal article. If you teach the course in this way, the major assignment will require the students to write up some portion of their recent or current research in the form of a journal article. Tell them this in the first session so that they may select a suitable set of experimental results by the time you next meet with them. The program presupposes that your students already have a year or more of research experience, and indeed we believe that this is the earliest stage at which students can profit from the kind of training described here. If the assignment suggested is impossible or inappropriate for your students, the "Notes on Major Assignment," p. 14, may help you to modify it.

The same belief in concreteness has led us to the piece of advice given at the head of this chapter: keep the introductory material short and get on to the steps in Chapter 2 within your first session. Those who have come unwillingly or skeptically to sample your course will not be won over by abstract argument about the importance of writing, but will almost certainly be intrigued by the first steps, especially the discussion of "What Is the Most Suitable Journal?", and will come back for more. Eager students will already be convinced that they want to improve their writing, and will be impatient to begin.

The instruction on the journal article (Chapters 2–8) has been designed according to the cardinal principle of Logic Before Language. There is a great deal more to writing an article than arranging well-chosen words in a clear, concise way. Before you introduce the dread word Style you must dwell long and thoroughly on how to define and delimit a topic, how to select some and exclude other experimental results, how to group ideas, how to arrange tables and figures, and how to write an outline. Some of these topics will be familiar to you from general treatises on writing; others are relevant to scientific writing only, and even for the more general topics many of the approaches suggested here for teaching them are unorthodox.

The order in which the topics are dealt with has been deliberately designed for palatability to the scientist. He is interested primarily in logical connections, so talk about logic and organization first. No one will be surprised as you develop the theme that only logical reasoning can produce a satisfying structure for the article. Then, when you have your students' full confidence, lead them gradually to the realization that the *same kind* of logical reasoning can yield precision and clarity in each sentence of the finished manuscript. In this way they will come, via paths that appeal to them, to an interest in words and their relationships. They will come to recognize that words are the coin in which we exchange thought, and that discussion of words in this context constitutes not a literary exercise, but a truly scientific activity.

2

The Ground Plan

YOU WILL NEED:

Copies of a few leading journals, some of wide scope (e.g., *Science, Nature, Journal of Biological Chemistry*), some of greater specialization (any high-quality subspecialty journals appropriate to your class). Choose the issues containing the Instructions to Authors or obtain copies of these for each journal.

One or two copies of *Current Contents* (Institute for Scientific Information, Philadelphia).

Trelease, S.F. *How to Write Scientific and Technical Papers.* 1969. The M.I.T. Press, Cambridge, MA. Recommend this as the textbook that deals best with *logical considerations* in scientific writing. Of the many published books on scientific writing, Trelease's is by far the pithiest, the most profound, and above all the most scientific. It is noteworthy that the first publication of this book in 1958 was the outcome of over 30 years of Trelease's refining of his earlier books on the subject published from 1925 onwards.

Since Trelease's own writing is highly condensed, students may find it a little indigestible if read at a sitting. A good plan is, therefore, to send them to the relevant passage only after you have expounded it vividly, with examples, in class.

YOU SHOULD READ:

Chapter 14 (pp. 167–178) of this book, as background for Step 3 (p. 13), not for transmission in detail.

O'Connor, M. and Woodford, F.P. *Writing Scientific Papers in English.* 1978. Pitman, London (first published 1975 by Associated Scientific Publishers, Amsterdam).

TIMING:

With Chapter 1, this chapter up to the end of Step 3 (including discussion) takes one hour.

ASSIGNMENTS:

Writing an abstract of a major article in a field appropriate to the students' interests. It is desirable to select an article that has either an unsatisfactory published abstract or no abstract at all.

Obtaining the Instructions to Authors (containing "Purpose and Scope") for a journal of the student's choice.

Any complex, large-scale task, which may be overwhelming to the beginner in its entirety, becomes more manageable when broken down into parts. The task of writing a journal article has therefore been broken down into about two dozen small steps, each of them rather quickly completed, which are described in this and subsequent chapters. Obviously, you may wish to increase this number, to skip lightly over some steps, or to rearrange them according to your own experience. They are listed in Table 1, page 9.

Stress the Two-Way Relationship Between Thinking and Writing

As you will inevitably find yourself constantly returning to one principle throughout the course, it might as well be discussed at the outset. It is that thinking and writing mutually interact. Good scientific writing is, of course, impossible without clear thinking. What is less obvious and less widely appreciated is that careful writing can actually assist in developing logical scientific thought. Somehow the discipline of crystallizing a thought into a grammatical sentence with a beginning, a middle, and an end clarifies, sharpens, and delimits that thought. You will find ample opportunity to demonstrate this useful feedback effect of writing (see, for example, Steps 2 and 5 below), and will be astonished how rapidly your students' power of clear, precise thinking will develop as they utilize it.

Several of the steps, including the first four, take the form of questions that the student is to ask himself.

STEP 1:   *What Is the Right Time to Publish?*

Graduate students who have not yet published find this an unexpected question. All the better, for one cannot impress upon them too early or too forcibly that good reasons must be given before they add a single drop to the flood of publication. Some scientists seem to believe that the world will be perpetually grateful to them for keeping what amounts to a public diary

TABLE 1   *Steps in Writing a Journal Article*

Step	Title	Page
1	What is the right time to publish?	8
2	What question has been asked, and what are the conclusions?	10
3	What is the most suitable journal?	12
4	How are the findings related to the existing body of knowledge?	14
5	Write the title and synopsis	15
6	Reread the "Purpose and Scope" in the chosen journal	16
7	Read the Instructions to Authors	16
8	Decide on the basic form of the article	17
9	Stock the section reservoirs	18
10	Construct the tables and figures	19
11	Construct the topic outline	20
12	Construct the sentence outline	21
13	Think of the article as a unit; write the first draft continuously from beginning to end	23
14	The Introduction: keep it short	24
15	Construct the list of references as you go along	25
16	Materials and Methods section(s): include the right amount of detail	26
17	Results section: allow the data to speak for themselves	28
18	Discussion section: watch for symptoms of megalomania	29
19	Are major alterations necessary?	30
20	Polishing the style	33, 34
21	Give drawings to Illustration Department	104
22	Write title and abstract in final form	104
23	Reread the journal's instructions to authors before having the manuscript typed	106
24	Departmental review	107
25	Shelve the manuscript for a while	108

of their diligent activity, or endlessly titillated by accounts of their viola-
tions of each one of Nature's infinite number of maidenheads. Science does
not advance by the accumulation of facts gathered at random and published
with the fatuous justification that they may "shed light" on some as
yet nonexistent problem. Make the idea of such publication repugnant

to your class. If you suspect that they may be more moved by considerations of ambition than of altruism, stress that in the councils whose opinions really matter in the furtherance of their careers, a few good papers count for far more than an infinitude of shameful "potboilers."

Actual evidence of the unfavorable effects of rushing into print is presented in Allen's article "Why Are Research Grant Applications Disapproved?" (Allen, E. M. 1960. *Science.* 132: 1532), which reveals that 12.6 per cent of the rejected proposals in the sample examined were disapproved because the investigator's previously published work did not inspire confidence. Let your students weigh this against the witty but oversimplified catchphrase "Publish or perish," by which they are all too easily impressed. Remind them that the printed word is indelible and that, even in the face of pressure from superiors, their first duty is to safeguard their future reputations. You will, of course, give special and different consideration to the rare, reticent creature who actually must be encouraged to publish his excellent research.

Well, what *is* the right moment to publish? Ideally, when a research question of some importance has been asked and a convincing answer found. Sometimes the complete answer cannot be expected within five or ten years; then publication is justified when a sizable step toward that answer has been taken. Perhaps the best criterion is: has a significant advance in knowledge been made? Remind the members of your class that on this point they will have to satisfy not only their own consciences but also a group of critics who may be even sterner: the editors, editorial board, and reviewers of the scientific journal to which the article is submitted. A young scientist's first contact with publishing can be a shattering experience; try to transform it into an educational one by preparing him for the cold-eyed appraisal of his peers. More on the kind of preparation to provide is given in Chapter 9.

STEP 2:   *What Question Has Been Asked, and What Are the Conclusions?*

Step 1 has been occupied with pondering these questions, and now we apply the device of writing down the answers in order to tether the thoughts to solid ground. The device establishes exactly what the article will be about. Failure to do this leads to the kind of publication that is, alas, only too frequent—the one that impels the exasperated reader to ask "What on earth is the man driving at?" Furthermore, the written sentences define the article's limits. Frequently the researcher is occupied with a number of closely related questions. It is imperative that he decide *which* question or questions will be discussed; which data are relevant, therefore, and which must be excluded.

Emphasize especially the form of the heading of this section: "What question has been asked?" (or alternatively, "What hypothesis has been examined?"), not "What was the purpose of the research?" The latter question can lead to the formless "purpose" of "investigating such-and-such a process" or "gathering data concerned with such-and-such a phenomenon," which advances nobody in the pursuit of explicitness and definition.

> ASSIGNMENT You can help your students read, as well as write, more effectively if you encourage them to ask "What was the question, and what are the conclusions?" of every article they study. Your first assignment can give them practice in this—and simultaneously convey that this course is concerned more with scientific thinking than with niceties of literary style—if it consists in having them make an abstract of a published paper. To convey the full meaning and significance of a major paper in a stringently limited number of words (say between 100 and 200) constitutes a challenging intellectual exercise. Usually you will be able to select a paper that will be sufficiently comprehensible, for the purposes of the exercise, to all members of the class. A list of well-written articles in several biological fields is given in *BioScience*, 1964, 14:22–23. Perhaps the students should aim at improving on the informativeness of the published abstract, where there is one, in a version that is only two-thirds as long. The assignment should be completed before the second class meets.
>
> Much fruitful discussion can arise out of this assignment. Students are eager to exercise their critical judgment, and will come up with many (real or imagined) faults of omission and commission even in a fairly good article. Encourage them to turn this critical faculty on their own writing and to resolve never to commit these faults when their turn comes to publish. You will almost certainly find instances in which the students have misread the article. Sort out with them who was at fault—they or the author—and stress the importance of critical, *accurate* reading. You can, perhaps, circulate your own version of the abstract and ask them to improve upon it.
>
> Alternatively, you may choose not to comment on this assignment in detail, but to give the same assignment at the end of the course

in order to assess (and have the students judge for themselves) what progress has been made in critical reading and thinking, as well as in writing, as a result of the course.

STEP 3: *What Is the Most Suitable Journal?*

With the precise knowledge of the contents and scope of the proposed article gained in Step 2, the author is ready to consider where he will submit it. I realize that the advice to consider this question so early is unorthodox. Yet it is a commonplace that the effectiveness of any piece of writing is directly related to the writer's knowledge of the audience to whom it is addressed. Nothing is more discouraging, demoralizing, and time-wasting than to prepare an article for a journal that rejects it for inappropriateness of content. Conversely, nothing saves more time at every stage of the article's preparation than the clear knowledge of where it will be submitted and who is likely to read it.

> ASSIGNMENT Point out that all journals publish a statement of their purpose and scope, although not necessarily in every issue. Have your students name the journal in which they expect to publish their next (or first) article and require them to obtain and study the "purpose and scope" of that journal and of possible alternatives before embarking on their Major Assignment.

Ask your students by what criteria they would choose one journal over another. You will elicit (or may have to supply) such answers as the following, and can expand them by means of the questions in parentheses.

1. General quality and prestige. (How is this judged? Does the composition of the editorial board provide a clue? What are your supervisor's and colleagues' opinions? Can you judge by critical appraisal of the contents?)

2. Size of audience. (A statement of circulation appears annually in most U.S. journals; those that carry advertising usually have a circulation of 5,000 or more.)

3. Type of audience. (Are you interested in reaching specialists only, or a wide audience? Is this determined solely by the journal, or do present methods of scanning lists of titles and selecting articles from *any* journal make this consideration unimportant?)

4. Speed of publication. Point out the distinction between date of *receipt* of manuscripts by a journal and the date of their *acceptance* for publication. Many journals publish both dates, from which one can deduce the time taken for the editorial process, including any necessary revision by the author; further, by comparing the date of acceptance with the date of publication of the issue one can deduce the time taken for the "production" phase—composition, proofreading, printing, and binding.

5. Quality of photographic reproduction. (In what types of work is this important?)

At this juncture it is useful to review and expand the students' knowledge of primary journals and of their place in the whole scientific information process. Such knowledge facilitates students' use of the literature and of the library at all stages of their work. It also enables them to write a primary journal article more intelligently, because they are aware that it is the fundamental unit of scientific communication, which is built into a more complex system by several means (publication of the abstract, discussion in other journal articles, citation in reviews, incorporation into textbooks). Your students should read the section "Guides to the Literature" in Trelease's book, pp. 11–25. List some questions to test your students' knowledge. What do they think are the criteria by which submitted manuscripts are judged? (In general, these include relevance to the journal's field, importance of the questions asked and the conclusions reached, strength of the experimental evidence, and clarity of presentation.) Do journals differ in the strictness with which they apply the criteria? What other considerations might be of overriding importance?

You can pull this discussion together, perhaps, by a practical suggestion for seeking a suitable journal in which to publish: scanning of *Current Contents*. The names of journals listed at the front of that publication will suggest that some of them should be examined further; since the titles of articles appearing in the current issue of those journals are reproduced inside, this can be conveniently done without extensive search in the library.

Notes on Major Assignment

It is unlikely that every member of your class has material ready to be published when your course begins. Encourage those who are not so far along either to select a small group of experiments, which is complete but which they would not normally consider (Step 1) a sufficiently important advance in knowledge to publish as a full paper; or to choose a portion of the work in progress that is incomplete, but for which a probable result can be predicted arbitrarily and appropriate conclusions drawn. The less artificial the exercise is, of course, the more effective it will be, but there need be nothing artificial about the second alternative I have described; in many types of experiments the experimenter knows beforehand that result A must lead to one conclusion and result B to another. Another possibility is to make the major assignment the description of a research proposal (see Chapter 12) concerned with work the student is embarking upon. Your important task is to ensure that the subject matter of the major assignment is research with which the student is personally involved.

Offer to discuss the choice of material for the assignment if the students have any difficulty in selecting it. Make sure that the choice is made early in the course and that the projected paper is small in scope, otherwise the student will have great difficulty keeping up with the steps as they are discussed in class. Once the material has been chosen, the student will require three weeks to complete Steps 1–12, when he will be ready to submit to you his sentence outline (see p. 21).

STEP 4: *How Are the Findings Related to the Existing Body of Knowledge?*

Once again, this is a step in which the author writes down what is presumably already fairly clear in his mind in order to clarify it further. What he writes specifies the *exact* area in which his advance has been made, where the work of others stopped short, and what the future developments could be. It eliminates irrelevant aspects of the field and prepares the ground for the Introduction and Discussion sections. Emphasize how precise you want this piece of thinking to be: one describes not the whole jigsaw puzzle of (say) amino acid metabolism, but only the pieces immediately surrounding the new knowledge concerning aspartate oxidation that is now to be fitted in.

STEP 5:   *Write the Title and Synopsis*

What a surprising piece of advice, your students will exclaim. People usually tell us to devise the title last! Furthermore, as to the synopsis, how can we give a general view of something that is not yet written? Explain that this is another piece of writing to clarify thinking. Although the title may well have to be revised when the article is finished, and the synopsis will almost certainly have to undergo a transformation before it can serve as an abstract, writing both of them at this point is invaluable to the author who is aiming for a tightly constructed article that is free from all irrelevance. And the student is, in fact, already perfectly well equipped to produce a working title and synopsis. He has a clear idea of what he has to say (Step 2), how it relates to previous knowledge (Step 4), and what constitutes his experimental evidence (in his notebooks); he is therefore in an excellent position to expound his projected paper in definite and concise terms, as though to a friend who asks him at some chilly street corner what he has been up to recently. The synopsis should be a logical chain of reasoning ("What was the question?"), observation ("What is the evidence?"), and deduction ("What are the conclusions?") without a single weak link in it. The author really defines the subject of his article and the limits he has set for it only when he has written a satisfactory title and synopsis. When this is done, he can feel that he has properly pegged out his ground plan and is free to move about comfortably within its well-defined limits as he plans the article in more detail and proceeds to its construction.

3

The Master Plan

You WILL NEED:

Copies of the Instructions to Authors in journals you deem appropriate.

TIMING:

Together with the last two steps in Chapter 2, a full hour.

ASSIGNMENT:

Steps 1–5 of the student's journal article (Major Assignment). Possibly, the reduction of a published article to outline form.

STEP 6: *Reread the "Purpose and Scope" in the Chosen Journal*

Now, with the subject matter firmly delineated on paper in the form of title and synopsis, the student should match it once more against the subject area of the journal he has chosen. This is his last chance to change his mind about the journal, for from here on all his words will be directed to that journal and to its readers. Because every line of communication has a receiving end as well as a transmitter, the successful writer is acutely aware of his audience. He must often decide, for example, "Should I explain this, or will my readers know it so well that they will be irritated by an explanation? On the other hand, can I find two or three words to bring in the less well-informed or less specialized reader without antagonizing the more sophisticated?" Such questions of judgment can be decided only if the student knows who his readers are likely to be. Study of the "Purpose and Scope" will aid his intelligent guesswork in that direction.

STEP 7: *Read the Instructions to Authors*

Ask your students what sort of information is contained in the Instructions to Authors that appear in most journals. Much of it is concerned with such mechanical matters as the number of copies to be submitted, spacing of lines, treatment of footnotes, etc., which will become important to the student only later. Nevertheless, even at this stage, it is necessary to know such things as whether there is a page limit (as in, for example, *Proc. Nat. Acad. Sci. USA* and *J. Exptl. Med.*); whether any style manual or other standard is adhered to for abbreviations; whether there are any special rules on nomenclature; and so on. Much time and patience can be needlessly expended on these matters if they are ignored until a later stage.

STEP 8: *Decide on the Basic Form of the Article*

Most scientific articles, at least in the life sciences, are arranged in four main sections: (a) Introduction, (b) Materials and Methods, (c) Results, and (d) Discussion. There are those who deplore this standardization, either because all uniformity is deadening or because it gives a false impression of an unimaginatively logical approach to scientific questions. Yet no one has authoritatively laid down this form; it evolved, early in the twentieth century, as scientific publication became more voluminous. It represents, I submit, a survival of the fittest among the various possible forms, where "fittest" means the most streamlined and efficient means of conveying information. It should be discarded, then, only when circumstances are absolutely compelling.

Obviously, material should not be forced into this mold when it does not fit—for example, a theoretical treatment of previously published results or a piece of work in which the reader must know the results of one portion before being introduced to the methods and experimental design of another. But the best advice to students is: use the conventional form whenever possible; if you adopt another one, do it in the conscious knowledge that some proved advantages of the conventional form will inevitably be lost, and satisfy yourself that there will be a net gain *beyond* the satisfaction of being unorthodox.

This is a good point at which to discuss the advantages of combining the Results and Discussion sections, together with the dangers. Any special forms, such as taxonomic descriptions, that are of special interest to your students should, of course, also be examined critically. You may also like to comment on how the Methods section has moved, at least in biochemical journals, from its former position as a sort of necessary appendix at the end of a paper to its present prominence near the beginning, and to explore the reasons. One is that the type of methods employed and the purity of substances used often have a profound effect on the results and on their interpretation. So important is this information that a further subdivision of the experimental section may become necessary, into a section headed "Materials" (in which the sources of both chemicals and biological tissue are stated and their purity is discussed) and another section headed "Methods."

In what follows, I have assumed that the conventional form has been adopted, but I do not mean to imply that no other is possible.

STEP 9: *Stock the Section Reservoirs*

A fundamental mistake of the inexperienced writer is to sit down with a rough mental outline of what he has to say, seize a pen with desperation and a groan, and start writing. At the end of the first page of botched sentences and confused thoughts, he is, not unnaturally, discouraged; only by great effort of will can he return to that distasteful pursuit—writing—and make another attempt.

It will by now have become apparent that this method is not the one advocated in this course. Because those scientists who are not "born writers" have no inherent pleasure in constructing a balanced sentence or a well-turned phrase, they should concentrate first on the things they do enjoy: facts, ideas, and logical connections. Tell your students, therefore, to take five sheets of paper; head them Introduction, Materials and Methods, Results, Discussion, and References; and into these reservoirs put—in any order they like—brief indications of facts, experiments, thoughts, and observations that belong in each. Naturally, the student's notebooks, graphs, card index, etc., should all be at hand to refresh his memory. The following considerations should influence his decisions on the items that are being added to the reservoirs:

(a) Is the item necessary? This is decided by reference to the title and synopsis, constructed in Step 5.

(b) In what section does the item belong? Some items may seem to have connections with two sections or even more; such items should be prominently marked, and the writer should consider carefully at this stage where they will be developed in most detail.

(c) Are all necessary items included?

As the work on the reservoirs continues, the structure of each section *and its relationship to the other sections* begin to emerge. More than one possible structure for the article may suggest itself, and if the student numbers the items he can readily experiment with different logical arrangements. But before the topic outline is attempted, another extremely important step must be completed.

STEP 10:   *Construct the Tables and Figures*

The student will protest that he has already tabulated his data and drawn his graphs; this was how he knew that he was ready to publish (Step 1). Explain to him that he is now going to draw them up in a way that will be completely intelligible to others. This includes composing full titles and footnotes for the tables as well as legends for the figures and labels for the axes of graphs. The step has three objects.

First, if tables are cleverly designed and have informative titles and complete footnotes, and if figures can be comprehended at a glance and have intelligible legends, the reader can glean not only the results but also a great part of the experimental design without any reference to the text. In the final paper the tables and figures, together with the title and the abstract, should form a coherent story. Ask your students in what order they look at the various parts of a published article, and many of them will give you: title, abstract, figures, tables, introduction, discussion, results, methods. Now, if it is true that figures and tables are often examined before the text, they should not be dependent on the text for comprehensibility. Few authors seem to realize this; put your students among those few by training them to design tables and figures *in full* before a word of the text is written. The first object of this step is, then, to make tables and figures fully informative in themselves and to banish from their vicinity the irritating and usually unnecessary inscription "see text."

Second, the tables and figures give the author a sort of extended synopsis of the paper. This may modify ideas developed in Step 9 as to the best order of presentation and therefore be useful for the writing of the topic outline, Step 11.

Third, matching the data thus tabulated and graphed against the items in the Section Reservoirs will reveal whether the conclusions must be modified (or abandoned!) and whether more experimental work should be done before the work is ripe for publication. In either of these two cases, time will not be wasted in writing a paper that may never see the light of day or that will reflect no credit on the author if it does.

These points about tables and figures are further elaborated in Chapter 10, but I think they are best discussed in detail after the students have already made mistakes and scored successes in designing tables and figures in the course of writing their major assignment.

Class discussion of Step 10 and its purposes will bring home to the students how useful it is to begin "writing" a journal article (using Steps 1–10) when a piece of research is *nearing* completion instead of when it seems to be finished. The steps reveal more concretely than vague daydreaming just what further evidence remains to be garnered. Recommend this to your students as a useful technique of research.

STEP 11:   *Construct the Topic Outline*

Let us assume that all is well and that further experimental work seems unnecessary. Now, I think, the author will be straining at the bit to put the items down in logical order—for it is really exciting to see the paper assume definite and logical form in the mind's eye. I defy anyone who is the least bit interested in his results to be untouched by this excitement as all the items in his reservoirs, tables, and figures seem to be jostling one another in eagerness to be put in place.

The topics should be arranged, within each section, in a logical order. What does this mean? Obviously, many different things. In Methods, perhaps a chronological handling of samples; in Results, the most important and explicable findings first, less clearcut differences later, or a gradation from simple to complex systems, or a discussion organ by organ, chemical class by chemical class; and so on. Some of these possibilities will be touched upon in subsequent steps, but, in general, scientists are strong in and proud of their logical thinking, and your students should be encouraged to display their prowess to the full. Point out the usefulness of headings, subheadings, and sub-subheadings as initial guides in writing even if they are scrapped in the final version; and stress how important it is to ensure that the ranking is logically correct, i.e., that a topic given a heading is really on the same level of importance as another that has been assigned a heading of the same magnitude. The longer the article, the more need there is for subheadings to guide both author and reader. You might add, parenthetically, that the doctoral dissertation must be strictly ordered by means of them, and that erroneous ranking is one of the major sources of confusion both in expository writing and in thinking.

The writer should make certain that he has included in his topic outline everything that was in his reservoirs and that repetition has been eliminated or minimized before he goes on to expand this outline in the next step.

STEP 12: *Construct the Sentence Outline*

Not all writers agree that a sentence outline is necessary, but its construction can be a further aid in clarifying thought for the neophyte. "How does it differ from a topic outline?" the students (rather to my surprise) ask. Whereas the topic outline defines what subject will be discussed in each section or paragraph, the sentence outline expresses what the writer has to say about that subject. Ideally, each sentence summarizes one paragraph in the finished article—shorn, of course, of all detail and supporting arguments—and the succession of sentences should make some sense to another person (allowing for the fact that transitional sentences may be necessary for complete intelligibility).

A sentence outline confers many benefits. It may, for instance, reveal gaps in the logic, even though the topic outline seemed perfect: perhaps a new heading should be inserted or the material rearranged. Sentences in the outline sometimes turn out to be so informative and pithy that the author delightedly extracts them bodily and uses them as key sentences in paragraphs of the final article. Finally, the construction of sentences prepares the writer for the phase of more continuous writing that is to come. Despite all these potential benefits, however, some writers find the sentence outline cumbersome and constricting. I ask my students to try it out experimentally, but not to force themselves to use it if it does not seem to help.

> ASSIGNMENT Description of these steps goes more quickly than their execution, and your students will be ready at this stage to tackle only the Ground Plan on their major assignment. I suggest that you give them three weeks in all to reach Step 12 (first week, Steps 1–5; second week, Steps 6–10; third week, Steps 11 and 12). Only at Step 12 is it meaningful for you to examine their work (a Topic Outline is virtually incomprehensible to anyone but its author). In my experience, science students perform well in the "outline" assignments, and for this reason you may like to bolster their confidence by giving them an additional

one to prepare. Ask them to take a published article (perhaps the one they have already abstracted at Step 2) and break it down into topic and sentence outlines.

You will realize that this assignment, like the abstracting one, is just the reverse of composing something as a *preparation* for writing a full text. Like a chemical compound, writing is more fully understood after it has been both analyzed and synthesized than after either analysis or synthesis alone.

4

The First Draft

YOU WILL NEED:

Copies of a good Introduction to hand out: either the one given on p. 25 or one of your own choosing.

Copies of a description of experimental methods, to be condensed into a form suitable for journal publication.

YOU SHOULD READ:

Trelease, pp. 36–42.

Gensler, W. J., and K. D. Gensler. *Writing Guide for Chemists.* 1961. McGraw-Hill, New York. Chapters 4 and 5 (from reference libraries; the book is out of print)

TIMING:

About 1½ one-hour sessions.

ASSIGNMENTS:

Condensation of a description of experimental methods.
Steps 6–10 of the student's journal article.

STEP 13: *Think of the Article as a Unit; Write the First Draft Continuously from Beginning to End*

A prime object of good style is unity. Unity should not be difficult to achieve in a journal article, written as it is around a single theme or research problem. If you know what you have to say, the article will flow best and be most coherent if it is written with one swing from beginning to end. Of course, *no* writer can achieve perfection as he goes along: the precise word, the clinching phrase are not at one's beck and call—sometimes, in the heat of composition, one cannot even decide how to end a sentence grammatically, let alone tellingly! But such obstacles should not deter the writer of a first draft. He should plunge forward, intent on the mainstream of his message, comforting himself with the thought that careful revision will smooth out the rough passages. In later drafts, the passage may be jettisoned altogether—why streamline something you will throw away? The main objective should be to get down some sort of account of each of the essential points, in the order indicated by the Sentence Outline. Some steering aids are offered in the following steps, which give specific help in different sections of the journal article.

Sometimes the reluctant writer is advised differently. He is encouraged to tackle the easiest sections first, complete them, and experience the satisfaction of having them safely under his belt. But the easiest sections are undoubtedly the Methods and Results, and as these are preceded only by a short Introduction, which serves to orient the writer as well as the reader, I believe that this advice is not so different from mine after all. The danger of writing separately conceived sections is that of producing a "patchwork quilt" of unrelated parts that no amount of patient stitching will unify.

Most of this advice applies exclusively to short articles with a single theme, such as will be forthcoming from your students at this stage. Long articles are perforce written in several sessions, but if the student has acquired the habit of writing his first drafts quickly, without editing, he stands a better chance of reducing the number of those days when writing goes painfully and unsatisfactorily. He will be relying on a *method* and not on inspiration.

STEP 14: *The Introduction*

The key direction to give here is: *keep it short*. Some scientists deplore the disappearance of the scholarly historical introduction from scientific articles. Certainly the young scientist's frequent lack of historical perspective may be partly due to the brevity of most present-day introductions—and this may be a good moment to disabuse your students' minds of the notion that science began ten years ago. But most readers, and certainly all editors, have tired of the lengthy account of the glorious advances of the past, to which the author's modest contribution seems to be attached in the hope of gaining luster by association. With the proliferation of review articles, the necessity for an extensive introductory survey has passed. The writer must, of course, know the history of his subject thoroughly, but his knowledge will be revealed by the way he describes his own work; there is no need to demonstrate it in any other way. He should select from that knowledge just enough to orient the reader adequately and to place the work to be described in appropriate perspective.

Good introductions often fall into three parts, be they sentences or paragraphs. The first states the general field of interest. The second presents, in main lines only, the findings of others that will be challenged or developed. The third specifies the question to which the present paper is addressed. The third part may indicate by what means the question has been examined, especially if the methods are new or unfamiliar, and may or may not state the conclusions, as the author wishes. The aim throughout should be to excite and interest, not bore, the reader, and answer the question: "Why was this work embarked upon?"

Choose one or two good Introductions to distribute and discuss. Here is one (Dobbing, J. 1963. "The Entry of Cholesterol into Rat Brain During Development." *J. Neurochem.* 10:739. Reproduced by permission of the author and of Pergamon Press).

"Previous experiments have shown a remarkable persistence of cholesterol laid down at the time of myelination in the chick and rabbit brain. In these experiments cholesterol-4-^{14}C was injected into the yolk sac of day-old chicks and intraperitoneally into 17-day-old rabbits (1, 2). It was recovered from the brain up to one year later, labeled in the same place in the molecule and at no other (3).

"An incidental finding was that the cholesterol molecule itself could enter the developing brain, although brain cholesterol has hitherto been considered to be entirely derived from synthesis within the organ. This new finding has recently been challenged in experiments with rats (4).

"In the present work rats have again been used in case there should be an unexpected species difference. The experiments were undertaken to determine (a) whether cholesterol as such could enter the brain; and if so (b) whether its rate of entry was as dependent on the timing of myelination as is the entry of other myelin-sheath constituents and their precursors."

S T E P   1 5 :   *Construct the List of References As You Go Along*

This piece of advice can be interjected here because the student is now actually writing the text of his article, albeit only in first draft. An unfortunately common practice is to mutter "I shall refer here to that article of so-and-so's in 1963" and to leave the "library work" to the very end. I have seen this cause more anguish than it is possible to describe. With the deadline for submission of the article two days away, the distracted author finds that half the necessary volumes are lost, borrowed, or at the bindery. All this is avoided if the writer, every time he refers to others' work, makes sure that he has the necessary reference in his files. Then, as soon as the momentum of his writing slackens, he must put down on a separate sheet, headed References, the full bibliographic details with all the authors' names, initials, and so on (is the title also required by the journal?), *in the style adopted by the journal of choice*. The references can be renumbered and rearranged later, if necessary, and their accuracy can be checked at any time, without panic, by consultation of the original in the library as the first draft nears its completion. Emphasize the importance of absolute accuracy, and make sure that your students know what the essential constituents of a reference are, namely:

For a journal reference: all authors with initials, journal title appropriately abbreviated (as recommended by the American and British Standards Institutes: see ANSI Z39.5-1969 (R1974) and BS 4148: part 2: 1975), volume, year, initial page (some journals require inclusive pagination), sometimes title of article. For books: author(s) with initials, title of book, editor(s) if any, number of the edition if applicable, publisher, city and year of publication, volume number if necessary, page number or inclusive pagination.

STEP 16: *Materials and Methods Section(s)*

The editors of some journals dislike, as I do, the word "Experimental" as a section heading. In no other circumstances is an adjective used as a heading, so why here? Most journals will accept the more specific heading Materials and Methods, even if their usual custom is to use the unfortunate "Experimental."

Common sense dictates when Materials and Methods should be described in separate sections, for example when the materials used are numerous and their purification is complex or particularly important. When experimental animals are used, the species and strain should be specified accurately. "Monkey" is an insufficient description in a scientific article.

Considerable delicacy of judgment is required to decide exactly how much information should be offered in the Materials and Methods section. All scientists are agreed on the principle that sufficient detail must be provided to permit the reader to repeat the experiments if he wants to. However, we must define carefully who "the reader" is. For these purposes, he must be assumed to be a trained investigator with considerable experience; otherwise, the article will become intolerably long and begin to resemble a manual of laboratory practice. The writer should ask himself constantly: "Is the average reader who is likely to want to do this work already familiar with this kind of manipulation? Are these details essential to the success of the experiment?" That the author may make the wrong decision on such questions does not absolve him from asking them and giving the best answer he can. Train your students to *include the right amount of detail.*

Apart from this, the Methods section is an easy one. The logical sequence has already been decided in the Outlines. It often follows a chronological pattern, e.g., chemical reaction conditions—purification of the product—analysis; or, treatment of animals—dissection of tissues—incubation conditions—assays—statistical methods for examination of results. Sometimes a succession of techniques, such as different types of chromatography, can form the different subheadings. Warn your students, however, of the perils of this approach if it conflicts with a chronological description, and point out how confusing it is to describe the analysis of a mixture which has yet to be extracted, or measurements on a substance of which the purification has yet to be described.

A frequent question is: "If I have used someone else's method for doing something, should I describe it or merely give a reference?" I believe that, unless the method is widely familiar (such as the method of Lowry, Rosebrough, Farr, and Randall for protein determination), the reader always appreciates being told at least the principle on which the method is based. Similarly, if the author has modified the method quoted he should give at least the outline of the modification. Modifications too trivial to be described are also too trivial to be mentioned.

> ASSIGNMENT Practice in exercising judgment about what to include and what to leave out when writing the Methods section can be provided in the following assignment, which also brings out a potentially useful distinction between the traditional "dissertation style" and that of a journal (see, however, Chapter 11). Ask your students to

condense the methods section of a dissertation to which you have access into a form suitable for a journal article. Good examples of this exercise in the field of preparative organic chemistry, in extended and condensed form, are given in Gensler and Gensler (see bibliography at the head of this chapter).

You may like to explore one technique for stimulating fruitful discussion of this assignment. Divide the class into groups of about five students and have them select and defend to the rest of the class what they consider to be the best condensed version. The critical analysis that is required brings home vividly the strengths and weaknesses of the version selected.

STEP 17: *Results Section*

The Results section should also be an easy one. The commonest fault here is to repeat in tedious prose what is already clear to the reader from a cursory examination of the tables and figures. If these have been well constructed, they will expose both the results and the experimental design (see Step 10). Little remains, then, but to make the object of each experiment clear in the text; to point out salient features, e.g., that A is greater than B (without giving the values), that something is linear over a certain range of concentration, or what the pH optimum is; and to connect the results with one another. In short, advise your students to *allow the data to speak for themselves* and to remember that the busy reader will be grateful for a guiding hand but should not be led as though blindfolded.

Authorities differ on whether the Results section should contain any conclusions. Some readers prefer to draw their own conclusions, without being prejudiced by the author, and compare them with the author's when they come to the Discussion section. If, however, the author keeps his Results section untainted by conclusions only to be forced to restate his findings in order to make the Discussion intelligible, he has avoided Scylla only to be drawn into Charybdis, for repetitiveness is a sin indeed. The best guide to offer is, perhaps, that the Results section must be comprehensible on its own and should indicate at least the *trend* of the author's reasoning, but that any extended discussion of the observations or comparison with others' work is best deferred until the last section. If no extended discussion is contemplated, the sections should be combined.

S T E P 1 8 : *Discussion Section*

This section is often the heart of a paper, the section in which the author assesses the meaning of his results. One can understand, then, why howls of protest go up when an editor suggests shortening it. However, the author should recognize that the minute consideration of every aspect of his work may not be as intensely interesting to others as it is to him, and there is a grave danger, if he indulges himself in a too-particular contemplation of nonessentials, that his reader may leave him before he has reached the nub of his argument. Again, he should realize that his natural desire to score off another investigator is only of marginal interest to the reader (unless he be that investigator) and, anyway, the pages of a journal are not the best place for personal rivalry. Try this as a piece of advice, then: *watch for symptoms of megalomania.*

Controversial issues should be discussed lucidly and fairly. Where results differ from previous ones, an explanation rather than a refutation should be sought. Anomalous results for which no explanation is readily available should be stressed rather than concealed, and the anomalies frankly admitted. Most interesting and valuable to science are the results which open up new possibilities of exploration, and these should be brought to the fore. Of course, *speculation* is in order in a Discussion, but it must be reasonable, firmly founded in observation, and subject to test, if it is to get past a responsible editorial board. A single hypothesis to explain results is almost mandatory, but piling hypothesis upon hypothesis is bad for the reader's digestion and the author's reputation. Sometimes the claim is made that some reader, somewhere, may be stimulated by the groping theories of an author, who should therefore not be forced to be too cut-and-dried. I think this notion is often grossly exaggerated. Only a very conceited man will seriously consider that science cannot advance unless his haphazard conjectures are enshrined in hallowed print.

5
The First Revision:
Structural Alterations

YOU WILL NEED:
Short versions of the "Condensation of Methods Section" assignment.

YOU SHOULD REREAD:
Trelease, pp. 44–46.

TIMING:
½–¾ hour.

ASSIGNMENT:
Steps 11, 12 of the student's journal article.

Revision of the first draft is best carried out in two distinct stages, described in Steps 19 and 20. In general, the less experienced the author, the more revisions are likely to be necessary; possibly, each of the following fractions of steps (subsumed under 19 and 20) may lead to a fresh draft. Teach your students not to be ashamed of four, five, or even more drafts— the greatest authors, whose prose looks as if it flowed effortlessly onto the page, have confessed to anywhere from 8 to 39 drafts before they were satisfied. Since perfection in the subtleties of literary style is not our aim, less revision than this should suffice, especially if it is logically directed and systematically undertaken.

STEP 19: *Are Major Alterations Necessary?*

Offer here four pieces of advice, given in the following order.

(a) SEEK OUT LOGICAL FLAWS

The ways in which a scientist can delude himself into believing that a cherished hypothesis has been proved are many and various. Trelease, pp. 44–46, trenchantly describes the most common ones. Of course, the purpose of all the hard thinking that went into the construction of the outlines was to avoid the possibility of any catastrophic failure of logic, so we shall expect the major argument to stand up without trouble. But there may be minor lines of reasoning that will not survive close scrutiny. Advise your students, therefore, to read those three pages of Trelease's book with the closest possible attention (the passage is so succinctly written that each sentence yields its full import only if one reads it two or three times and ponders it well). They should then consider every statement and inference in their first draft, sentence by sentence, for faults of logic. Few things give a better training in scientific method than the ruthless examination of one's own statements in the light of well-defined principles.

(b) CORRECT ANY MISQUOTATIONS

The writer should inspect with particular care his statements about others' work. Impress on your students that they must reread at this point the papers or passages of papers cited in the first draft and acquit themselves of any suspicion of misinterpretation—for an author's prejudices only too readily distort his remembrance of an earlier worker's conclusions. Students should guard even more carefully against the common tendency to cite a finding that has no true bearing on the point under discussion but merely relates to the same complex of ideas. Quoting out of context to give an impression different from that intended is, of course, universally condemned.

I doubt very much that the writer who commits these offenses does so in a deliberate attempt to deceive. The errors come from self-deception and wishful thinking, from a false recollection, or from notes that are too sketchy. Above all, the writer should recognize that his frame of reference has almost certainly changed since he first planned his research and read the articles cited. He owes it to his readers, and even more to himself, to read the articles again in the light of his present knowledge and attitudes and to assure himself that he is not quoting them incorrectly in either the letter or the spirit. For whatever the motives or reasons behind misquotation, the consequences are always unfortunate: knowledgeable readers (including editors and reviewers) lose confidence in the writer's competence, while the ignorant are misled.

To those who grumble that it is immense labor to read all that literature again, be merciless. Scholarship is not compatible with laziness, and science cannot progress where sloppy thinking is condoned. To put forward a hypothesis without checking the accuracy of the supporting arguments is like determining the composition of reaction products without being sure that the starting materials are pure.

You may wish to suggest this examination of the cited literature at an earlier stage—Step 11: Construct the Topic Outline. But I believe that this advice is valuable only to scientists with considerable experience in writing journal articles. Indeed, in planning the Introduction and Discussion, such writers should reexamine the leading sources of the arguments they will employ there. Novices, though, are all too easily distracted and discouraged from the task of writing their first drafts, and this rereading of published work may provide merely another tempting excuse for procrastination. If the reevaluation comes after the first draft has been written, the author has gained some confidence in his ability to write and is therefore willing to face the task of remodeling, should this seem called for.

(c) REEXAMINE THE ORDER OF PRESENTATION

Even if no changes under (a) and (b) seem necessary, and even though Topic and Sentence Outlines were constructed and dutifully followed, make the student take a long, hard look at the first draft and consider whether it is soundly designed. He should ask himself in particular: "Will the function of each section be clear to any reader on his very first approach?"

Since clarity of purpose is the key to unity and coherence, the student should now refresh his memory about the exact intent of the article he is preparing, by reference to his title and synopsis. His main object at this stage is to ensure that the paths of reasoning in the first draft, rough and stony though they may be at present, at least point resolutely toward the goals he has defined.

If work on the Outlines has been thorough, shifting of material from one section to another should not, of course, be necessary. But miscalculations are always possible. The very process of writing the first draft may have revealed that a more logical development would result if facts and ideas were rearranged within the original framework. If so, now is the time for the scissors and paste—not later, for then the arduous dovetailing of each sentence to fit its context would have to be undertaken twice.

(d) Combine or Simplify Tables Where Necessary

A closer look at the tables drawn up in Step 10 may now reveal that portions of them are irrelevant to the point being made, or that two or more of them can be combined to increase comprehensibility. Similarly, graphs may profitably be reconstituted to convey their message more directly or vividly. Some principles that should underlie this revision are given in Chapter 10.

Step 19 has been largely concerned with logic and structure. When any major alterations necessitated by this step have been made, and not before, the student can proceed to the correction and improvement of style.

STEP 20: *Polishing the Style*

Style is probably what your students expected, in a course on writing, to hear about from the start. A few will have been disappointed not to have heard it mentioned, but most will have been relieved that you have been primarily concerned with something familiar and dear to them—scientific method. These need not feel they are entering foreign territory even now, if you emphasize that good scientific style consists of these qualities:

> rational construction of sentence and paragraph (*logic* again);
> absolute accuracy of expression (*precision*);
> ready comprehensibility (*clarity*);
> *directness*; and
> *brevity*.

Thus the scientific writer need strive only to be logical, precise, clear, direct, and brief. Most desiderata of literary style—for example, grace, mystery, urbanity, wit, lightness, word-music, rhythm—are, although not necessarily undesirable, inessential here. I think you will have little difficulty in persuading your students of the importance and desirability of good style *as thus defined.* For their greater comfort, stress that good scientific style can be learned: it is a craft rather than an art—by which I mean that it demands no special inspiration, or genius, that stamps a man as different from all others. Such inspiration, in a scientist, will have manifested itself at an earlier stage of the work: in the choice of problem, the experimental design, and the deductions. These you do not pretend to teach.

The discussion of scientific style (Chapter 6) will occupy at least three complete sessions, so it will constitute a considerable apparent digression from the numbered series of steps. You may like, therefore, to state at this time what the remaining steps will be (Chapter 8), in order to convey the feeling that completion of the task is somewhere in sight.

6

Further Revision: Polishing the Style

The over-all plan for the sessions on style that constitute Step 20 is as follows.

First session: consideration of the true aims of style in scientific writing; enunciation of four principles of scientific style, with examples; assignment of sentences and phrases for correction.

Second session: consideration in class of answers to the assignments; discussion of points of special difficulty and any necessary amplification; discussion of the recommended reading list; and distribution of the "editing assignment"—a complete, badly written paper for correction (see Chapter 7).

Third session: correction of the "editing assignment" in class, preferably with the help of an overhead projector. After this, students should be able to proceed to apply the stylistic principles to the revision of their First Draft.

This schema should be flexible: four sessions may be needed.

You will need:

First Session
1. Copies of the book list, p. 56 (to be discussed in the Second Session; you will, however, refer to it in the first). This is a suggested *short* list to be handed out to your students; for full bibliography for your own reference, see the beginning of each chapter and the Bibliography of Further Reading, p. 179.
2. Copies of assignments related to each of the principles of style discussed (for suggested assignments see pp. 42, 48, 52, and 54).
3. Desk copies of (for full bibliographic details see p. 56): Fowler (*Modern English Usage*); Gowers (*The Complete Plain Words*); Strunk and White (*The Elements of Style*); Quiller-Couch (*The Art of Writing*); Baker, J. R. English style in scientific papers. *Nature*. 1955; 176:851–2.

Second Session
1. As above, plus copies of Baker's article for distribution.
2. Duplicated lists of the "Warning Words," see p. 51.
3. Copies of the Editing Assignment (see Chapter 7; have only the faulty text on the left-hand pages duplicated, with the superscript numbers omitted and with each line numbered for easy reference. See pp. 55 and 57 for preparation of alternative editing assignments).

Third Session
Transparent (Diops) copies of item 3 under Second Session.

Y OU SHOULD READ:

All the books on the students' book list, p. 56.
The recommended passages on p. 42.
Fowler (*Modern English Usage*): entries headed "Unattached participles"; "Participles"; "Fused participles."
Booth, V. *Communication in Science: Writing and Speaking.* 1984. Cambridge University Press, New York and Cambridge.
King. L.S. *Why Not Say It Clearly: A Guide to Scientific Writing.* 1978. Little, Brown and Co., Boston.

S T E P 2 0 :   [*First Session*]

THE AIMS OF SCIENTIFIC STYLE

All that you have told your students up to now has laid a firm *foundation* for good scientific style, for it has been concerned with clear, logical thinking. Getting one's thoughts in good order is one of the hardest tasks in the world, especially if they are complex, novel, and exciting, and there will have been little chance during the preparation of the first draft to hunt and trap the telling word or to perfect the economical phrase. Now comes the time to polish the style.

Make it plain from the start that "style" is not an ornament applied to the outside of something essentially simple in order to dress it up for greater impressiveness. Stylistic improvement in scientific writing goes, generally, in quite the opposite direction. Explain that you will first bring to your students' notice some of the common faults of style in scientific literature, and then show how they can be avoided.

Define here what you mean by faults of style: impediments to the transfer of ideas. Ideally, sentences should be smooth; but if the price of smoothness is ambiguity, something clumsier but unequivocal is better. Brevity, we have said, is desirable; yet a long, precise statement is always preferable to a concise one that is inexact. In other words, the students should aim not at superficial graces but at functional beauty. To do so they must know what the function of scientific prose is: to convey logically ordered ideas exactly, concisely, and clearly.

There are many excellent books full of advice on how to achieve clarity in writing (see the bibliography, pp. 179–184). You will do well to commend Strunk's classic above all others. Strunk is concerned also, as are Gowers and Quiller-Couch, with directness and vigor. These are indeed admirable qualities in expository writing. But a goal that is rarely stressed in general books on writing, one that is of particular importance in science and of particular appeal to scientists (for obvious and good reasons), is precision. You should not hesitate to stress this special quality in *scientific* writing, both as a desideratum and as a strong suit in the scientist's hand.

However excellent the texts that you encourage your students to read may be, the words of wisdom will not take root unless their meaning is brought home by a great deal of practice. Numerous assignments that will provide this practice are offered to you here. Elementary faults are dealt with first, in single sentences or phrases, and more subtle and interesting ones are presented later in the Editing Assignment (Chapter 7), in which the student polishes the style of an entire article.

Obviously, the discussion of style must have a well-defined structure if it is not to degenerate into the consideration of a multitude of single instances from which no precepts emerge. I suggest a framework of four stylistic principles to supply this structure. A detailed description of each of them is given below. These principles have not been conceived in vacuo, but have emerged from my own experience in editing scientific articles. They are not infallible, and can and should be violated when there are overriding reasons for doing so. For that reason they are best regarded as principles rather than rules, although it is simpler and shorter to refer to Rule 1, Rule 2, and so on.

Make clear that you do not mean that the "rules" should impose some restriction on the author's style from without; rather, good style grows from within as the principles are first understood, then applied, and finally transcended. The principles do not by any means supply the answer to every stylistic problem, but if the student learns and understands them thoroughly he will have acquired a writing technique that has a firm basis. Most important of all, by studying and applying these principles the students learn a *method* for criticizing their own writing. The method involves rational consideration of the purposes of writing, the application of well-defined principles, and the constant reappraisal of "rules" given here and elsewhere. What could be more congenial to a research scientist?

First, warn your students *not* to aim for the currently accepted style of scientific writing. They should *not* study the leading journal in their specialty and attempt to imitate the writing it contains. Unfortunately, there has grown up among scientists a ritualistic mode of expression that is at once grandiose and alien to science's grand purpose—which is surely explanation, not obfuscation. To combat this false style, arm your students for the fray with these firm intentions: to think straight, to say what they mean, and to ensure by constant consideration of their audience that what they say will be understood. Encourage them to treasure their native directness, and to spurn, not imitate, the tortured prose of others.

Fowler and Fowler begin their classic, *The King's English*, with this powerful sentence: "Any one who wishes to become a good writer should endeavour, before he allows himself to be tempted by the more showy qualities, to be direct, simple, brief, vigorous, and lucid." This admonition applies to all expository writing, but as we have seen, scientific writing demands one other quality: precision. The following enunciation and discussion of four principles of scientific style show, with examples, how Fowler and Fowler's five characteristics—and the additional characteristic, precision—can be attained in scientific writing. The resultant prose is, in functional beauty, as far beyond the tortured Gothic outpourings of current scientific writing as the buildings of Mies van der Rohe are beyond those of the (original) Smithsonian Institution.

Rule 1, *Be Simple and Concise*, works toward being "direct, simple, brief" and combats the tendency of the immature writer to be bombastic and verbose. Rule 2, *Make Sure of the Meaning of Every Word*, aims at precision; the rigorous application of this simple principle can not only increase accuracy of thought but also eradicate most of the grammatical faults common in scientific writing. Rule 3, *Use Verbs instead of Abstract Nouns*, enables your students to write more vigorously. Finally, their writing becomes both more precise and more lucid if they *Break Up Noun Clusters and Stacked Modifiers* (Rule 4), which creep so insidiously into the hasty or thoughtless writer's work. Let us see, then, how these rules can be imparted and how they work out in practice.

RULE 1: BE SIMPLE AND CONCISE

This most fundamental rule of expository writing can be introduced, if you will, by a delightful anecdote from Plutarch. It illustrates that from ancient times thoughtful men were aware of the danger of letting their tongues run away with them. "Anacharsis, when he had been feasted and entertained at Solon's house and lay down to sleep, was seen to have his left hand placed upon his private parts, but his right hand upon his mouth; for he believed, quite rightly, that the tongue needs the stronger restraint."

What was Anacharsis afraid of? That if he allowed himself to babble, some secret might be revealed. If a writer allows himself to babble in print, an even greater secret may come out: that he is not quite sure what he is talking about. He may have become so lost in impressive, orotund phrases that he is no longer able to face the issues squarely. One sure way to come to grips with a line of reasoning and examine whether it is logical is to express it in the simplest possible terms. For his own sake, then, as well as for the reader's, the writer should check through the first draft of his text—word by word and sentence by sentence—with these questions: "What can be shortened or simplified? What can be eliminated altogether?" The time and hard work it takes to substitute the simple expression for a long-winded circumlocution are well invested, for the more practice the writer gets in simplifying his expressions, the clearer and more forceful become his vocabulary and his thinking.

One of the worst faults of current scientific writing is a kind of hypnotic prolixity. The reader of a scientific article often gets the uneasy feeling that it describes a rite, in which the investigators Jones, Smith, and Robinson circle solemnly among the crucibles, ecstatically intoning

"Optimal reaction conditions are approximated when . . .";

"In studies pertaining to the identification of phenolic derivatives, drying of the paper gives less satisfactory visualization";

and

"Insufficient data are at present available to completely negate the possibility that removal of the abovementioned substances from the circulation is not a factor of importance."

These are (real, not invented!) examples of *jargon*, the kind of magniloquent utterance that the specialist falls into when he forgets to strive for simplicity. The etymology of "jargon" is revealing: it is derived from a medieval French word meaning the warbling, twittering, and chattering of birds, and has the same root as "gargle." Jargon consists, then, of sounds that are meaningless. It often results when words are borrowed from one scholarly vocabulary, where they have a precise meaning, and used, in another discipline, in a pseudo-scholarly way. Thus "to approximate" has a precise meaning in mathematics, but the first of the above examples ("Optimal conditions are approximated when . . .") does not use this meaning (of continuous approach to an ideal, or ultimate value)*; the ornamental flourish actually says no more than "The reaction goes fastest when. . ." (Or does the phrase mean "The reaction goes most nearly to completion when. . ."? Simple language enforces accurate *thinking*.) Thus, the writer is not merely verbose; he is inaccurate.

Impress upon your students with all the vigor at your command how dangerous an inflated style is, not merely in obscuring meaning for the reader but in so veiling the issue from the *writer* that the chances of his making a blunder are greatly increased.

The second ritualistic example,

"In studies pertaining to the identification of phenolic derivatives, drying of the paper gives less satisfactory visualization,"

may seem innocuous to those of your students whose sensibilities have already become calloused by daily contact with scientific writing at its present low standard. Ask them if they don't prefer

"Phenolic derivatives are more easily seen and identified if the paper is left wet."

Some may be so far corrupted as to be shocked by the "bluntness" of the restatement. Others will admit that they prefer it, but object that it may not be what the author meant. This objection brings out a prime justification for simplifying high-flown passages: they are usually ambiguous. Still others may feel that although the simpler form communicates more easily and vividly, the difference is slight. Get these objectors to realize that a writer who permits himself one such pompous sentence will almost certainly persist in his stylelessness, constantly being complex where he could be simple. Each small, unnecessary effort of comprehension the reader must

---

* Writers have become so careless in thinking about the meaning of words that I have recently seen "The amount of X was approximated by . . ." when the writer meant "estimated" or "determined"!

make tires and frets him, and lessens his receptiveness even if he escapes being consciously bored.

You can draw here an analogy between the writer and an archer who points his bow at a target (the reader's comprehension) a hundred yards away. It is the archer's responsibility to trim his arrows and take his aim, not the target's to swell so that it can be hit. An error of a centimeter at the firing end means a yard off the bull's eye. The real danger is that complacency about such poor aim, such small lapses into unnecessary complexity, quickly leads to monstrosities like the "insufficient data" sentence above or to:

"A variety of stimulatory hormones, irrespective of their chemical nature, are characterized by their ability to influence the synthesis of messenger RNA as a prerequisite for the secondary biologic events characteristic of the particular target organ."

Have your students rewrite this sentence in simple prose, and discover for themselves how little they understand it, how wide of the mark its author was.

At this point, you may have to counter students' protestations that you seem to be opposed to the use of technical terms. Naturally, you are not. Technical terms are often polysyllabic, yet they are concise because they have precise (if often complex) meanings that would require many more words to convey in any other way. But in habituating ourselves to these polysyllabic terms we become inclined to use other polysyllabic words and phrases that sound dignified but that turn out on examination to be merely pretentious. In the bad sentence above, the only technical term is "messenger RNA"—and this is the clearest feature of the whole sentence! Give your class a common example of fuzziness induced by nontechnical verbiage: "under conditions of high pH." This says no more than "when the pH is high." Why bury pH, which says so much so succinctly, under the woolly blanket-word "conditions"? Encourage your students to develop and use a "thinking man's vocabulary," not the jargon of the pseudo-intellectual. "A man of true science uses but few hard words, and those only when none other will answer his purpose; whereas the smatterer in science thinks that by mouthing hard words he proves that he understands hard things." (Herman Melville)

You may also have to counter another kind of objection. Certain fields engender a special terminology, which, the students say, is perfectly well understood and indeed is a useful shorthand way of conveying information within the charmed circle of its most active practitioners. They admit that it may be misunderstood by outsiders, but suspect that they may not become accepted members of the "in-group" if they fail to follow the leaders' example. Calm their fears on this score. Even "club members" are susceptible to the appeal of clear, simple English and will never even notice when jargon is missing. Ask your students if they want to reach *only* the members of the in-group. Are they bent on repelling others? Do they want their papers to have lasting value, or are they content to see them become quickly outmoded because of the perishable cargo of vogue words they bear? Discourage them, too, from the propagation of neologisms. A little thought, and a little dictionary work, will often produce an exactly equivalent, already existing, English word to substitute for their uncalled-for brain-child.

I have, in contrast to the authors of many books on style, put simplicity and conciseness together under one heading, for I believe they should be aimed at *simultaneously*. Otherwise a whole group of students will produce, in a laudable attempt only to be simple, this kind of verbose passage:

"The numbers of enucleated cells in vaccinated and nonvaccinated mice were determined both at four and eight days after inoculation and (or) the beginning of fasting. The number of enucleated cells in vaccinated mice was seen to be greater than in nonvaccinated mice and to increase from four to eight days after inoculation, whereas the number of such cells examined under the same conditions in nonvaccinated mice actually decreased during the first part of the experimental period and then increased from four to eight days, but not to the same extent as they did in mice that were both vaccinated and fasted. Consideration of the numbers of enucleated cells in all four groups, see Table 1, reveals that the effect of fasting seems to have been superimposed upon the effect of prior vaccination, at least in the second portion of the experimental period."

As Strunk puts it, "conciseness requires not that the writer make all his sentences short, or that he avoid all detail and treat his subjects only in outline, but that *every word tell*" (his Rule 13, p. 17). Few words tell in this "simple" passage, which is therefore as tedious to read as if it had been wrapped up in polysyllabic elaborations.

Further invaluable reading on what constitutes nontechnical jargon is to be found in the following (for complete references see p. 56):

1. Gowers, *The Complete Plain Words*. Recommend that your students read at least *case* (pp. 58–9), *position, situation, conditions,* and *level* (pp. 208–210). The last-named has acquired enormous popularity with the development of molecular genetics (use of such phrases as *at the transcription level* has led to absurd imitations like *at the membrane level,* where *level* is completely superfluous). Ask them what they would think if you told them that you are dealing with writing *at the ideational level.*

2. Strunk and White, Rules 12 (p. 15) and 13 (p. 17).

3. Quiller-Couch, Chapter V, "On jargon." This classic deserves to be learned by heart.

4. Baker's two-page paper, see beginning of this chapter.

Show your students, by requiring them to read these short excerpts, how entertaining books on style can be. It is not sufficient to place the books on a "recommended reading" list—you must whet the students' appetite for them.

A list of complicated sentences for simplification and condensation is given below. Indubitably you can supplement this list from your current reading.

EXERCISES ON RULE 1 (with suggested corrections)

This phenomenon is associated, in a causative or accompanying way, with . . .

    (This phenomenon causes or accompanies)

At the termination of the experiment . . .

    (At the end of the experiment)

. . . has the capability of . . .

    (can, is able to)

. . . at a high speed level . . .

    (quickly, rapidly)

This result would seem to indicate the possible presence of . . .

    (This result indicates that . . . may be present.)

Effectiveness of the oral inoculum in producing caries varies widely with the strain of rat; in some cases, rats may become highly caries active, whereas in other strains, the oral inoculum has much less adverse influence.

    (delete everything after the semicolon)

X produced an inhibitory effect on the formation of Y.

    (X inhibited the formation of Y.)

It was possible to obtain semipreparative (100 μg) quantities of substance X.

    (About 100 μg of X could be made.)

X formed Y at least an order of magnitude faster when . . .

    (X formed Y at least ten times faster when)

Computations were conducted . . .
> (Calculations were made; or, X was calculated)

. . . in a state of protrusion . . .
> (protruding)

. . . subsequent to their entry into the cell . . .
> (after they have entered the cell)

. . . occupies a juxta-nuclear position . . .
> (is next to the nucleus)

Solvents were pre-cooled at 0°C prior to use.
> (What does "pre-cooled" have over "cooled," or "prior to" over "before"?)

One lot contained particles greater than 74 μ, and this material was shaken on a sieve prior to use to remove particles in excess of this size.
> (One lot contained particles *larger* than 74 μ; these were removed by sieving.)

Figs. 1–3 are photographs of thin-layer chromatograms developed in the solvent system described and are typical of the separations achieved with this chromatographic method.
> (Figs. 1–3 show typical chromatograms.)

RULE 2: MAKE SURE OF THE MEANING OF EVERY WORD

"Alice had not the slightest idea what Latitude was, or Longitude either, but she thought they were nice grand words to say."

Science is full of nice grand words, and very tempting to tongue and pen they are. But if a major objective of our writing, as of all our scientific activity, is precision, we must use them with the greatest care. If we try to write without understanding their meaning *exactly*, it is like trying to obtain a result with uncalibrated equipment, while revision is like trying to find a fault in the equipment without understanding the basic principles of its construction. Insist, then, that your students calibrate their equipment by frequent recourse to dictionaries (for words of general meaning) and to textbooks (for definitions of technical terms).

Be patient with your students. They entered quite suddenly, at college, a world of ideas peopled with a vast number of new words, some of which were never adequately explained, many of which are inaccurately used in the articles they read. The only adequate corrective is constant vigilance and a conscious appraisal of each word that they write. Ask them to consider (as examples of precision in word usage) whether enzyme reactions are studied in solutions of *varying enzyme concentration* or in solutions of *various enzyme concentrations*. Is a *variety of improvements* reported, or are *various improvements* described? Did the clinician administer *varied* treatments or merely *different* ones? Are two values *equivalent* or *equal*? What is wrong with "Both methods yielded similar results," or with "The adsorption is completed in 15 minutes. This greatly reduces previously reported adsorption times."?

Your students may not be as patient with you as you are with them. "Oh, for pity's sake," they cry, "we know just what the fellow means, why all the pedantic fuss?" Convince them that this apparently robust, commonsense attitude is, in fact, a nonscientific one, analogous to that of a housewife who cannot conceive that an ounce of butter one way or the other is going to make the slightest difference in her cooking, whereas the scientist frequently encounters the case in which a milligram and even a microgram makes all the difference in the world. Anyway, *is* the reader so sure what "the fellow means"? If the writer's prose abounds in minor inaccuracies like this, we *cannot* be confident that when he refers to "10 mM glucose . . . in a total of 3 ml" he actually used 3 ml of a 10 millimolar solution. The carelessness of his style makes it distressingly likely that he made a common error of abbreviation and actually meant "10 millimoles of glucose per 3 ml of solution." The 300-fold difference might well be crucial in an experiment.

For precision of diction, a knowledge of definitions is (of course) not enough. Besides the meanings of individual words, the writer must examine words *in context* to ensure that the correct meaning is conveyed. An intelligent university student without any formal knowledge of grammar can actually correct most faults in grammar simply by analyzing his sentences logically. Can anyone fail to spot the error in "This value was found by Smith in rabbits who reported that . . . ," provided he is examining the meaning of every word and its context? Nevertheless, an awareness of common pitfalls is helpful. One such pitfall is the unattached or dangling participle; another, the dangling infinitive; a third, the omission of auxiliary verbs. A brief discussion of these points is worthwhile (although you may feel that continuity is best preserved if you defer this to the *second* style session). A treatment such as the following is suitable.

Dangling participles.   Scientific writing abounds in dangling participles because it is difficult to combine successfully the frequently used (and useful) passive voice with a participial construction. As you know, a verbform (participle or infinitive) is said to "dangle" when the (unstated) subject of the verb in question is *not* the subject of the main clause of the sentence.

A dangling participial construction may be unobjectionable ("The experiment was performed using redistilled solvents"), misleading ("Chromatography fractions were sampled, followed by UV measurement, and dried."), or downright ludicrous: "After closing the incision, the animal was placed in a restraining cage" (skillful surgeons, some of these laboratory animals!). Baker, in the article in *Nature* cited at the head of this chapter, states that "anyone who is intelligent enough to carry out scientific research at a university can easily grasp everything that it is essential to know about the use of present participles and gerunds in fifteen minutes." Although Dr. Baker may be optimistic, do give your students fifteen minutes of instruction on the point. As source material use Fowler on *Unattached participles*, the excellent example given by Baker, and horrid examples you have collected yourself. Recommend these simple precepts to be applied in revision of the first draft:

(a) In each sentence, establish the subject of every verb (in whatever form the verb may appear—active or passive voice, participle, infinitive). Ensure that the subject, if present, is unequivocally in the right context or, if absent or represented by a pronoun, is unambiguously implied.

(b) Distrust all words that end in "...ing" and examine their context for correctness (see Fowler on *Participles*, esp. *Fused participles*). Particularly avoid *following*, which is usually a clumsy elaboration for *after* but which sounds distressingly like a participle, to the confusion of all ("The milkiness of the intestinal lymphatics of a *dog following a fat meal*...". Poor, starved animal! "Following the meeting in Paris, the editors visited London." How vague about a rendezvous can you get?)

Dangling infinitives. These are almost as common as dangling participles. Take, for example, the sentence "The flask was flushed with nitrogen to remove ozone." The intended subject of the verb "remove" is "the experimenter," but this subject is not mentioned. *Grammatically*, therefore, the implied subject of that verb must be the subject of the main clause—"flask"—and the nonsensical inference to be drawn is that the flask wanted to remove its excess ozone. The fault is *not* corrected by inserting "in order," since these words merely elucidate that the infinitive is an infinitive of purpose and do not essentially change the grammatical structure. Nor is the fault corrected by inverting the sentence to "Excess ozone was removed by flushing the flask with nitrogen," for then we have a dangling *participle*, "flushing" (grammatically, the ozone must be doing the flushing).

The best correction in most instances of this kind is to insert the true subject of all the verbs, namely "we," and transform the sentence into the active voice. "We flushed the flask with nitrogen (in order) to remove excess ozone" or "We removed excess ozone by flushing the flask with nitrogen." If the passive is considered essential, the possibilities (cumbersome but correct) are: "The flask was flushed with nitrogen and the excess ozone thereby removed"; "Flushing the flask with nitrogen removed excess ozone" (here the notion of *purpose* is not expressed, but is rather obvious; "flushing" in *this* sentence is not a participle but a gerund or verb-noun); and "In order that excess ozone might be removed, the flask was flushed with nitrogen."

Omitted auxiliaries. Avoidance of the repetition of "was" or "were" in a sentence—a device applied by many writers, perhaps in an unconscious attempt to decrease wordiness—requires careful handling if the sentence is to emerge grammatically correct. The following classification of omitted auxiliaries is readily understood and applied:

(a) *Invariably incorrect.* Two different verbs and two different subjects, one of which is singular and the other plural, e.g., "The rats were killed and their blood pooled." (Blood were pooled??)

(b) *Sometimes correct, rarely advisable.* Two (or more) verbs, each with its own subject, all subjects being singular (or all being plural): "The dog was anesthetized, blood drawn through a long needle provided with anticoagulant, and serum separated by centrifuging." Although grammatically correct, this kind of sentence plunges the reader into a succession of uncertainties. Are we supposed to read "blood drawn through a long needle was provided with anticoagulant" or "blood was drawn through a long needle [that had been] provided with anticoagulant"? Did the serum separate or was it separated? Insertion of "was" at two points would remove all doubts.

(c) *Always correct and desirable.* One subject, and a string of verbs, e.g., "The solution was warmed, stirred, decanted, and evaporated."

The writer (and reviser) can guard against errors that result from omitting auxiliaries if he again follows the advice (see above): establish the subject of each verb and ensure that its context is correct.

In general, it is not appropriate to deal with any other points of grammar in a course of this sort. Individual students who need grammatical help or study can be directed to such textbooks and workbooks as that by Jones and Keene (see the annotated bibliography beginning on p. 179). Chapter 19 of their book provides particularly appropriate examples and exercises on parallel construction, agreement of subject and verb, reference of pronouns, dangling, trailing, and misplaced modifiers, and other grammatical problems. Tichy (see students' book list, p. 56) deals with the matter of grammar sensibly, by reviewing only the kinds of mistake that are common in *scientists'* writing. It may amuse you to discover what a large proportion of the faults she lists can be detected by a conscientious reviser who applies Rule 2—to take two common examples, the unidentified or ambiguous antecedent of pronouns (detected by "what is the meaning of *it* or *this* here?") and the nonagreement of subject and verb (detected by "what is the meaning of the context of this verb, i.e., what is its subject?"). Your whole approach should be, I think, to get your students to rely on logical analysis for the removal of blemishes, rather than to give a full review of formal grammar.

Detailed analysis for meaning will often turn up scientific solecisms such as the following:

"The solvents were evaporated in vacuo at 40°C under a stream of nitrogen."

Here the author has been too lazy to examine the meaning of the words "in vacuo" that are daily on his lips—shouldn't this phrase be banished forever in favor of "at reduced pressure" if there is any danger of its leading to the absurdity of specifying that a vacuum shall be composed of nitrogen? Unmasking blunders such as this constitutes, surely, the whole justification for detailed criticism of one's writing.

Urge your students, then, to combine common sense with their not-so-common intelligence and to acquire an ingrained habit of ruthless word-by-word criticism. The ultimate object will be to make every sentence (as Quintilian put it) not merely capable of being understood, but incapable of being misunderstood. No writer, least of all a scientist, should lay himself open to the kind of reprimand that Alice received:

"Speak English!" said the Eaglet. "I don't know the meaning of half those long words, and, what's more, I don't believe you do either."

EXERCISES ON RULE 2

Ferric chloride was deleted from the color reagent.

(simple malapropism of "deleted" for "eliminated" or "omitted")

Glyceryl ethers of varying degrees of unsaturation . . .

(The continuous "varying" is inappropriately used instead of "various.")

A method is described for use on unfractionated human plasma that is superior to that now in use.

(Is the *plasma* superior to that now in use?)

The composition of the lymph of the fasted rat is also unlike depot fat.

(Is the composition unlike *fat*? This is a very common type of fault, eliminated by inserting "that of" before "depot fat.")

The addition of hexokinase decreased palmitate oxidation and was therefore not included in the incubation medium.

(The *addition* was not included?)

The optimal conditions for transesterification approximate those for phospholipase activity.

(not "approximate," which means "approach," but "are about the same as")

The two major components analyzed very close to that expected for the mono- and diacetate structures.

(1. Did the components analyze, or were they analyzed? 2. What is antecedent of "that"? 3. What is the use of the word "structures"?)

The problem of diffusion constants of almost insoluble substances . . .

(Are diffusion constants a problem?)

Due to the low resistance of the plate, a 100-ohm resistance was placed in series with it.

("Due to" is often advantageously replaced by "because of." Try inverting the sentence: it makes sense with "because of" but not with "due to.")

Following the incubation, the remaining fluid was poured off and the slices washed.

(1. Was the fluid following the incubation? Use "after." 2. The auxiliary verb "were" is omitted.)

The tubes were shaken, followed by centrifugation, and the upper phase withdrawn.

(Were the tubes followed by centrifugation? Were the upper phase withdrawn?)

Fasting blood was drawn.

(Can blood fast?)

In view of the colored nature of retinol . . .

(What is a colored nature? Can it come into view, as a color can?)

Based on electrophoretic patterns, hyperlipoproteinemias have been classified.

(Were hyperlipoproteinemias based on electrophoretic patterns?)

Other investigators have reported large populations of lactobacilli in fecal contents. Reference 7 presents a recent review dealing with this problem.

(Are large populations—at least in this context—a problem?)

In the steady state, the daily fecal excretion of neutral plus acidic steroids of endogenous origin should approximate the daily synthesis of cholesterol.

(. . . should approximately equal . . .)

Contrast this correct usage:

When radioactive cholesterol is given to patients with every meal, the specific activity of biliary bile acids approximates that of plasma cholesterol after some days.

and point out the strength and utility of precise vocabulary and usage.

Rule 3: Use Verbs instead of Abstract Nouns

So far we have talked about being simple, brief, logical, and precise. Writing that has these characteristics can still be unappealing: noble and virtuous, perhaps, but lifeless. The Fowler brothers knew what they were about when they commended vigor as a prime characteristic of good writing. Lucas, too, remarks that it is not much use making your reader see, if you also make him yawn.

What is it that makes most scientific writing so preeminently dull? I believe it is the failure to use expressive verbs, for the best way to bring a piece of flabby writing to life is to use richly meaningful, telling verbs. Yet scientists seem to want to weaken the verb in every possible way. They show an inexplicable urge to use gerunds, abstract nouns derived from verbs, or noun-phrases—anything *but* a verb, in fact—to do the work in a sentence, which then has to be grammatically completed (since a sentence, by definition, demands a verb) by some pale shadow of a verb like "effected." Thus, instead of the vigorous "A was separated from B" we have to suffer "The separation of A from B was effected." The force of the verb "separate" has been dissipated by its transmutation into "separation." Your first task is, then, to train your students to recognize and then *release the hidden verb*, that sleeping beauty so often locked up in a bland ivory tower of an abstract noun.

Mention of the abstract noun brings up a second aspect of this principle of using verbs: it enables the writer to substitute concrete action for hazy abstractions, which, as every professional writer from antiquity to the present knows, is vital to holding your readers' interest. In scientific writing we are often dealing with, and necessarily writing about, abstract concepts.

All the more reason, then, to write concretely when no abstract idea is being put forward.

> "Isolation of the tertiary component was accomplished and its identification achieved by the following sequence of manipulations."

Here the scientist is not thinking, like some yearning recluse, of the accomplishment of isolation; he is thinking, and should be writing, about isolating a particular compound. Nor is he concerned, like a spiritual guru, with the ultimate achievement of identification; he just wants to identify a single chemical. When actions are earthbound, their description should be earthy —and vigorous.

The technique of releasing the hidden verb leads, as your best students will already have realized, not only to greater vigor but also to simplicity and brevity. Circumlocution is often the result of burying verbs in other, longer parts of speech (not "explain" but "is explanatory of"; not "results from" but "is the resultant of"). In addition, using verbs instead of nouns can lead to greater precision, because the proper use of a verb forces the writer to specify subject and object unequivocally. Abstract nouns allow the subject to remain unnamed and insubstantial, which is why the writer of official documents loves them so (see Gowers). In one example I encountered, I was able to conclude only after diligent search of the context that the sentence "Repeat aspiration was necessitated" probably meant "The upper layer had to be siphoned off twice"; I remained uncertain, however, since the subject "the upper layer" had not been specified.

Your advice will be, then, to release hidden verbs wherever feasible; but you will find that your students need much practice before they can recognize nouns (and other parts of speech) derived from verbs. A useful aid in doing so is to compile and keep at hand a list of "warning words" which usually indicate a nearby trapped verb in distress. These warning words are the colorless shadows of verbs I mentioned above as being necessary to complete the sentence in which an abstract verb-noun lurks: "carried out," "effected," "achieved," "facilitated," and the like. A list of them appears in Table 1. I suggest distributing this list in the Second Session, but you may prefer to do so here. Do not call them "forbidden words," because in some contexts they are inevitable and right. But they should be memorized as warning signals. When the student finds one of them as he revises his first draft, he should stop at once and examine the sentence closely. Can it be expressed more succinctly, precisely, directly, vigorously? Almost always he will discover that it can.

TABLE 1 *"Warning Words"*

These are to be regarded not as invariably undesirable words, but as warning signals that something may be amiss, or susceptible of improvement. One soon gets into the habit of noticing them at a glance, on any page.

Colorless verbs (usually to be eliminated; they occur most commonly as the past participle, as shown)

accomplished	experienced	obtained
achieved	facilitated	occurred
attained	given	performed
carried out	implemented	proceeded
conducted	indicated	produced
done	involved	required
effected	made	

Woolly words (sometimes these have a precise meaning; more often, they are an indication that the thought has to be sharpened)

area	problem
character	process
conditions	situation
field	structure
level	system
nature	

Words incorrectly used as synonyms

amount	alternate	minimal	varying
concentration	alternative	negligible	various
content		slight	varied
level			different

Dangling words
All words that end in "ing" or "ed" and all infinitives

Danger words

this (obscure antecedent)	their, its, and all
it (obscure antecedent)	other pronouns

Vague qualifiers (can usually be omitted, since they add nothing)

fairly   quite   rather   several   very   much

EXERCISES ON RULE 3

Protein determinations were performed as described above.

(Proteins were determined as described above.)

Hydriodic acid attack on unsaturated ethers proceeds at olefinic bonds.

(Hydriodic acid attacks unsaturated ethers at olefinic bonds.)

Conversion of acetates to iodides was effected.

(Acetates were converted to iodides.)

Primary and secondary particle separation was obtained by performing electrophoresis.

(Primary and secondary particles were separated by electrophoresis. "Performing" is both dangling and redundant.)

Injection of the protein was more difficult of achievement in older animals due to the frequency of occurrence of thrombosis.

(It was more difficult to inject the protein into older animals because thrombi often formed.)

Preferential release of monoenoic acids would also appear to be the case in man.

(Monoenoic acids seem to be preferentially released in man also.)

The separations were checked frequently to ensure that quantitative recovery of cholesteryl esters, uncontaminated by triglycerides, was being achieved in the second fraction.

(Frequent checks established that cholesteryl esters, uncontaminated by triglycerides, were recovered quantitatively in the second fraction.)

The paper lost its integrity.

(The paper disintegrated.)

There was predominantly protein formation . . .

(Proteins were mostly formed . . .)

RULE 4: BREAK UP NOUN CLUSTERS AND STACKED MODIFIERS

A factor that contributes significantly to the flexibility of English is that one noun can be used to modify another without any inflection. Thus, "disease of the liver" can be perfectly satisfactorily rendered as "liver disease" even though an adjectival form for liver, "hepatic," exists. When more than two nouns are gathered together, however, trouble begins. In "adult liver disease" we become uncertain which words are substantive and which modifying: is the writer referring to liver disease in the adult, or to disease of the adult liver? Here, perhaps, it does not greatly matter; the phrase makes sense whichever way you group the words, just as in "rabbit ear skin" or "serum cholesterol level." But when we encounter "liver disease plasma" the case is different. Does this mean "disease(d) plasma flowing through the liver," "hepatic plasma in disease"? No, the only meaningful combination seems to link the two first nouns to form a complex adjective and make the phrase mean "plasma obtained from patients with liver disease."

The meaning of these noun clusters can, then, usually be puzzled out—although sometimes a real, unresolvable ambiguity results, as in "heavy beef heart mitochondria protein" (which is heavy—the beef, the heart, the mitochondria, or the protein?). The major objection to noun clusters is that the writer has shown discourtesy in using a shorthand designation that may be convenient for him but is highly inconvenient for the reader.

The difficulty is compounded when not only a couple of nouns, but a whole string of modifiers, is cavalierly flung down before a single noun. Here real uncertainty arises as to what is meant to modify what. Except to an expert in the field, the meaning of "a radium containing argon ionization chamber" is totally obscure. Perhaps you think that a little reflection will unscramble this: the chamber, which contains radium, is a device for ionizing argon—why bother to add words spelling it out? My answer is twofold. First, the onus of making the translation should not be on the reader. Second, the translation is *wrong*: the chamber does contain both argon and radium, but the "ionization" is of organic vapors that enter the chamber and react with the electrically excited argon. So much for the attitude "Oh, they'll all know what I mean!"

If the reader is in as much of a hurry as the writer of such careless phrases, understanding may never be reached. In a paper in which a reader has become used to translating "silica gel coated glass fiber paper chromatography" into "chromatography on paper that is made out of glass fibers and coated with silica gel," "nonglucose light experiments" into "experiments carried out in the light in the absence of glucose," and "light glucose cells" into (believe it or not) "cells grown in the light in the presence of glucose," he will almost certainly be waiting for the main verb in "The presence of glucose delayed daughter cell release in 80% of experiments . . . ," only to discover after much cogitation that the main verb is actually there! The noun cluster consists of only three words, *daughter cell release*, and the sentence is meant to be read: "The presence of glucose delayed the release of daughter cells in 80% of experiments." Readers with this degree of perseverance are more than such an author deserves.

How should one detect clusters of nouns and modifiers, judge whether they impede communication, and correct them if they do? Detection is easy, if tedious. The student should pick out every noun in his draft and count the number of modifiers it bears. A useful rule of thumb to ensure lucidity is to allow the coupling of two nouns ("palmitate oxidation") but not the addition of a third ("sheep palmitate oxidation") nor even of a modifier of the two-noun cluster ("enhanced palmitate oxidation"). And the correction is also rather simple: decide the precise relationship of the modifiers to one another, and express this relationship by inserting prepositions and verbs. Some loss of brevity is inevitable, but lucidity is too important a commodity to be sacrificed on the altar of conciseness, and you should not allow your students to defend their clusters with Rule 1 as their banner. This is one example, out of many you will encounter, of the need to overrule one principle because of the greater importance of another.

EXERCISES ON RULE 4

The monoamine oxidase inhibitor insensitive agent
    (The agent that is insensitive to the inhibitor of monoamine oxidase)
Radioactive glycerol-labeled triglyceride metabolism
    (Metabolism of triglycerides labeled with radioactive glycerol)
Anomalous stability constant order
    (Anomalous order of stability constants)
. . . in order to obtain high purity, high yield aldehyde
    (. . . in order to obtain aldehyde in high purity and high yield)
Highly purified heavy beef heart mitochondria protein
    (Protein from the highly purified heavy fraction of bovine heart mitochondria)
Proteolipid protein-free lower phase lipids
    (Lipids contained in the lower phase, free from proteolipid protein)
Cellulose acetate electrophoresis procedure
    (Electrophoresis on cellulose acetate)

The minute analysis of imperfect prose that is necessary to illustrate principles such as the ones I have given may seem irksome. Elaboration of these points is indeed unnecessary to a naturally gifted writer, who instinctively avoids the kind of solecism I have discussed. But it is to the less gifted that our attention is directed, to the student who senses that something is wrong, but who does not know why, or how corrections can be made. He needs clearcut principles—principles he can see the point of, and believe in—to guide his hand and brain. If you can demonstrate that by application of these simple principles a passage is markedly improved, the student rapidly discovers that the process is exciting rather than tedious, and develops a style that is a worthy vehicle for the liveliness of his thought.

STEP 20: [*Second Session*]

After the students have wrestled with the short assignments, it is advisable to discuss the four principles again, with the aid of further examples, in order that the students not only grasp them but become thoroughly familiar with them. You can distribute the "Warning Words" (Table 1) as a basis for this amplification. The first part of the table lists colorless verbs and is to be related to Rule 3; the rest of the table refers to various aspects of Rule 2.

The grammatical points I discussed under Rule 2 (dangling constructions and omitted auxiliary verbs) can also now be considered.

Discuss the short book list (p. 56), distinguish between books to be read thoroughly and those to be used for reference, and ensure that the students have embarked on some reading of them. The "highly recommended" books can be described with enthusiasm to those of your students who have some literary bent and appreciation and who have already mastered the Four Rules, but do not launch into this encomium too early; the student must tangle with and overcome the fundamental difficulties before he can appreciate these elegant and eloquent pleas for better style. Even the lively book by Tichy, which is specifically directed toward scientists, should be regarded as the basis of *further* refinement of style rather than as an introductory text. One great strength of this appealing book is the wealth of examples in which scientist-writers have succeeded, in contrast to the many I have quoted who have failed, in the task of scientific communication.

Distribute the Editing Assignment (examples are provided in Chapter 7) and explain to your students that it is so loaded with faults that they will certainly have to rewrite every sentence, at least in part, and reorganize some of the paper as well. In particular, they should examine the Table for possible simplification, and consider whether any material should be moved from the Results to the Methods section or vice versa. Tell them that you will go over this paper in detail in the next session, but that they should correct it, as far as they are able, before then. Emphasize that they should read the faulty article right through before giving way to the natural urge to start correcting: only if the point of the article is understood will the editing be soundly based.

"Editing assignments" such as the examples I have given can be com-

BOOKS ON (SCIENTIFIC) WRITING

Essential textbooks:

Strunk, W., Jr. and White, E.B. *The Elements of Style*. 3rd ed. 1979. Macmillan, New York and London. Original (Strunk) copyrighted 1918.

Trelease, S. F. *How to Write Scientific and Technical Papers*. 1969. The M.I.T. Press, Cambridge, MA. Paperback issue of the 1958 publication by Williams and Wilkins, Baltimore, MD.

Reference works:

A good collegiate dictionary. Webster's is the most often referred to but is the most permissive; American Heritage is a better authority for educated usage. British writers will prefer the Shorter Oxford English Dictionary.

Fowler, H. W. *A Dictionary of Modern English Usage*. 2nd ed. 1965. Oxford University Press, Oxford and New York. (First published 1926.)

Partridge, E. *Usage and Abusage*. 1976. Penguin Books, Harmondsworth, Middlesex and Baltimore, MD. (First published 1946.)

Roget's Thesaurus. Innumerable versions, including paperback editions. (First published 1852.)

CBE Style Manual Committee. *CBE Style Manual*, 5th ed. 1983. Council of Biology Editors, Inc., Bethesda, MD.

Recommended:

Gowers, E. (revised by Fraser, B.) *The Complete Plain Words*. 2nd ed. 1973. HMSO, London. Paperback: Penguin Books, Harmondsworth (Mx) and Baltimore, 1970.

Huth, E. J. *How to Write and Publish Papers in the Medical Sciences*. 1982. ISI Press, Philadelphia.

Kane, T. S. and Peters, L. J. *Writing Prose: Techniques and Purposes*. 5th ed. 1980. Oxford University Press, London and New York.

Lock, S. *Thorne's Better Medical Writing*. 2nd ed. 1977. Wiley, New York and Chichester.

Lucas, F. L. *Style*. Cassell, London, 1955; Collier, New York, 1962; Pan, London, 1964. Currently out of print, but included here because it is worth searching out in libraries.

O'Connor, M. and Woodford, F.P. *Writing Scientific Papers in English*. 1978. Pitman, London.

Quiller-Couch, A. *The Art of Writing*. 1961 (reprint of 1946 edition). Folcroft Library, Folcroft, PA.

Tichy, H. J. 1966. *Effective Writing for Engineers, Managers, Scientists*. John Wiley and Sons, New York and Chichester.

posed very easily. You may want to prepare one whose subject-matter has closer appeal for your particular class. Just take any *short*, well-written, published paper—one of your own, for instance—and inject into it examples of all the faults that have been discussed in the preceding pages plus others that you find especially objectionable. This can be done rapidly if you have before you a list of "Warning Words"; the exercises on the Four Rules; and compilations of circumlocutions, passive constructions, malapropisms, and clichés such as are contained in "Expressions to Avoid" in O'Connor and Woodford's *Writing Scientific Papers in English*, pp. 93–98, or the *US Government Printing Office Style Manual* (Washington, DC, 1973).

STEP 20: [*Third Session*]

YOU WILL NEED:

A copy of the "editing assignment" distributed at the end of the Second Session, identical with the students' copies except that it is made on transparent Diops (sheets of clear plastic); a supply of sharpened wax pencils; and an overhead projector that throws onto a screen an image of the sheet and of your pencil as you make corrections.

If you do not have the facilities to have such Diops made, use an ordinary copy of the assignment and a projector such as is used for projecting an image of a page in a book. You will not be able to make corrections on the projected image, but you will be able to point to the offending words or passage. Make provision, in this case, for an illuminated blackboard, if possible, so that you can use it while the image of the page is still being projected in the darkened room.

Because the object of this exercise is not so much to arrive at an improved version of the faulty paper as to teach general principles of style, work out beforehand which of the corrections you will spend most time on and ensure that each one either makes a major point or can be related to one of the Four Rules already enunciated. It is discouraging for students to watch you make many minor corrections that seem to have no general application and no relationship to an over-all scheme. For the same reason, control the extensive discussion that inevitably results from this exercise in such a way that the framework of principles and the categorization of errors remain clearly in the foreground. Defend nothing on the grounds of personal taste; if you can refer neither to a principle of scientific style nor to an unequivocal rule of grammar, concede the point. Try to avoid being either pedantic or apologetic.

Your students will have detected and corrected many of the errors already, and will be heartened by seeing you treat them in the same way. Other points will be new to them. In some places, content yourself with indicating what is wrong, and why—and let your students provide the correction. As a final exercise on Style, have them extend and complete the editing of the assignment in the light of what they have learned during this session, and hand in their final version of it a few days later. A brief examination of these versions will show where each student still needs guidance or further study, and you will be able to direct him to appropriate authorities. Try not to involve yourself in detailed correction at this stage; such correction will be much more telling in the revised draft of the student's Major Assignment, to which he is more deeply committed both intellectually and emotionally.

STEP 20:   [*Fourth Session*]

You may or may not consider a fourth Style Session to be necessary; but it is wise to allow for it if possible. Your students will almost certainly be bursting with questions: they may want you to explain one of the principles again or to provide a more elegant solution than theirs to one of the problems in the editing assignment. On your side, you may want to elucidate something that they apparently have not grasped. Perhaps you should stress again the enjoyment and profit to be gained from careful reading of the books in the book list (p. 56) and the importance of *critical* reading of everything that comes their way for the continuing development of good scientific style.

After the editing assignment and subsequent session(s), return to the sequence of steps, in which *Step 20: Polishing the Style* has been a lengthy one, and fill in the details of Steps 21–25 as indicated in Chapter 8. You may wish to end your course there, or to extend it with the material in Chapter 9 or any of the chapters in the second half of this book that fit both the needs of your students and your own time schedule.

7

Editing Assignments

In this chapter three examples of "editing assignments" are given. For instructions on how to prepare and use such assignments, see Chapter 6.

None of the examples carries a heading abstract. Advise students, when you give them the faulty text to edit, to read the whole paper through and write an abstract of it—in order to establish for themselves what the paper actually has to say—before they begin to correct the style.

THE PROBLEM[1] OF LIPID PEROXIDES AS ARTIFACTS IN HUMAN AORTA LIPIDS

N. B. Gee, P. D. Cue, and S. O. Hess

INTRODUCTION

It has been suggested by some researchers[2] (1) that peroxides of lipids that are formed in the arterial wall conceivably[3] have a possible[3] role in causing[4] atherogenesis. This postulate has been widely accepted as a reasonable one, in view of the ready capability of breakdown of these compounds with the initiation of progressive chain reactions and the formation of a variety of[5] potentially toxic secondary[6] products.

In this connection,[7] the destructive effects of lipid peroxides on serum β-lipoproteins (2) and on the SH group in proteins (3) have been noted[8].

---

[1] Word frequently misused in scientific articles. Real chemical substances such as peroxides cannot be a "problem": the problem may be where they come from, how to get rid of them, or how to prevent their formation. Often a scientist will call something a problem which is actually a phenomenon ("The Problem of Adhesive Selectivity in Cellular Interactions"). The problem he has in mind, of course, is how to account for the phenomenon, but this is beside the point. (Rule 2)

[2] "by some researchers" redundant. (Rule 1)

[3] Triple hedging: "suggested" is already tentative enough; "conceivably" and "possible" weaken rather than strengthen the effect. (Rule 1)

[4] This word should never be thrown about incautiously. Here, it can simply be dropped (if we remember the precise meaning of "genesis"). (Rule 2)

[5] Common circumlocution. (Rule 1)

[6] The force of "secondary" is obscure. What is the difference from "primary" products? Are *only* the secondary products potentially toxic? These questions expose the word as verbiage. (Rule 2)

[7] A weak connective, to be used only in desperation. Should a new paragraph be started here? (Rule 1)

[8] This prissy word warns the alert reviser that there is something wrong: probably the "real" verb is hidden in some other word. And it is: "destructive." (Rule 1)

ASSIGNMENT 1: IMPROVED TEXT

THE ARTIFACTUAL NATURE OF LIPID PEROXIDES DETECTED IN EXTRACTS OF HUMAN AORTA

E. X. Celsior and I. M. Provement

INTRODUCTION

It has been suggested (1) that lipid peroxides formed in the arterial wall are[1] active in atherogenesis. The[2] suggestion[3] has been widely accepted as reasonable, since these compounds break down[4] readily, initiating chain reactions[5] as they do so and forming various products that are potentially toxic[6]. For example, lipid peroxides[7] denature[8] serum β-lipoproteins (2) and attack the SH group of proteins (3). When vitamin E-deficient

---

General. A good title should be short, informative, and precise, and much anxious thought should go into it both before the paper is outlined and after the final draft is ready.

This one is far from elegant. It starts with the article "The," which can often be dispensed with but which is essential here. It contains the warning word "nature." Re-examine the title after you have read the article, and decide whether it conveys the message exactly. If it does, further elegance need not be sought.

[1] How clear the air becomes when the triple hedges are torn down! But note: there is no diminution of caution. (Rule 1)

[2] Eliminate "this" whenever it is not strictly necessary. (Rule 1)

[3] A "postulate" is something assumed without proof. (Rule 2)

[4] Trapped verb in the abstract noun "breakdown" has been released; note increase of comprehensibility. (Rule 3)

[5] A chain reaction is always "progressive." (Rule 2)

[6] "Potentially toxic" rearranged to a position of emphasis. Word order is a subject for discussion on Further Points of Style; see Lucas pp. 39–41, 231 ff.

[7] No change in direction of ideas, hence no new paragraph.

[8] When the trapped verb in "destructive" has been released, the author finds that he wants to be more specific about the *kind* of destruction.

Lipid peroxides appear in rat adipose and muscular
tissues under conditions[9] of vitamin E deficiency
and during the application[10] of a diet rich in
polyunsaturated fats (4), and the formation[11]
of "ceroid" in atherosclerotic arteries has been
attributed to the autoxidation[11] and polymerization[11]
of the unsaturated lipids which they contain (5).
    Following[12] the results of Lufton and Sowerby
(1), the atherogenic role for lipid peroxides has
been on firmer ground[13]. They[14] found an increasing[15]
degree of lipid peroxidation in human aortic wall,
positively correlated with the degree of
atherosclerosis. It struck[16] us that the lipid
extracting method[17] used by them, namely mixing with
anhydrous sodium sulfate by means of a chop-knife
and extraction of the mixture with chloroform, was
liable[18] to effect[19] the artifactual formation of
lipid peroxides from unsaturated lipids, and we
undertook reinvestigation[20] of the lipid[21] peroxide[21]
occurrence[21] problem employing extraction[20] at greatly

[9] Warning word: the statement containing it may be vague. (Rule 1)
[10] Is a diet "applied" or "fed"? (Rule 2)
[11] Abstract nouns containing hidden or trapped verbs. (Rule 3)
[12] Eliminate "following" wherever possible. Sometimes it is a dangling participle, sometimes a vogue-word substituting for the simple "after." Here, as in many instances, it leads to the hilarious suspicion that the atherogenic role is following the results around (see Fowler: *Following*). (Rule 2)
[13] The metaphors "role" and "firm ground" are not dead enough to allow of mixing (see Orwell, G., 1947, "Politics and the English Language," *The New Republic*). (Rule 2)
[14] Antecedent ambiguous ("results," "Lufton and Sowerby," "peroxides"?) (Rule 2)
[15] Increasing with what? (Rule 2)
[16] Inappropriately colloquial.
[17] The scientific literature is riddled with this Germanic construction. In English it is sheer nonsense: what lipid ever extracted a method? Who ever asked in a drugstore for a coffee containing cup? (Rule 2)
[18] Anthropomorphic.
[19] An affected "warning word." (Rule 3)
[20] Abstract nouns for pomposity's sake. (Rule 3)
[21] Nouns clustering (Rule 4) around the foolish "problem."

rats are fed[9] a diet rich in polyunsaturated fats, lipid peroxides appear in their adipose and muscular tissues (4); similarly, it is thought, unsaturated lipids present in atherosclerotic arteries may autoxidize[10] and then polymerize[10] to form[10] "ceroid"[11] (5).

Lufton and Sowerby (1) provided some evidence[12] for the atherogenic role of lipid peroxides. They showed that the content of peroxides[13] in lipids extracted from the human aortic wall[14] increased[15] with the degree of atherosclerosis. They[16] extracted the lipids, however, by mixing the tissue[17], exposed to the air[18], with anhydrous sodium sulfate and extracting the mixture with chloroform at room temperature[18]. These treatments may have caused the artifactual formation, by oxidation[19], of peroxides from unsaturated lipids during the extraction. We have therefore reopened the question of whether lipid peroxides[20] occur in aorta lipids, using an—

[9] Reserve the frequently substituted "administered" for occasions when unnatural forms of feeding (e.g., stomach tube) have been used. (Rule 1)

[10] The trapped verbs "form," "autoxidize," and "polymerize" have been released. Note increase in simplicity and vigor. (Rule 3)

[11] "Ceroid" has been brought to a position of emphasis.

[12] The cliché "on firmer ground" has been substituted by the unobjectionable "evidence."

[13] The corrected version is more specific, i.e., avoids the abstract "peroxidation" and speaks of "peroxides." (Rule 3)

[14] Phrase expanded for clarity and precision.

[15] Simplification of "positively correlates" with no loss of meaning.

[16] This time "they" can open the sentence because antecedent is unambiguous. The construction, moreover, is now parallel to that of the preceding sentence.

[17] "the tissue" has been added for clarification (answering the question "mixing what? Lipids?"). (Rule 2)

[18] "exposed to the air" and "at room temperature" have been added to bring out why the method might have led to oxidation.

[19] Specific and informative expansion of "formation."

[20] Breaking up the noun cluster to give "the problem of the lipid peroxides" reveals that it is not so much a problem as a question; releasing the hidden verb "occur" produced the further simplification. Notice that the verb "occur," so often a colorless nothing-word, is here accurate and meaningful.

reduced[22] temperatures in order to achieve[23]
avoidance[20] of that possibility[20].

MATERIALS AND METHODS

Aortas were obtained at 6–12 hr autopsy[24] at the
University Hospital, Barchester. The classification
of each as regards stage of atherosclerosis (0, I,
II, or III) was done as described by Gee et al. (6),
examining[25] the appearance of the intima, after
which the adventitia (outer layer)[26] was rapidly but
carefully[27] removed.

The intima and media aorta preparations[28] were
immediately put into a mixture of methanol and
chloroform, approximately[29] 100 volumes, 2:1 (v/v).
Storage took place at –20 °C. Following[30] the lapse
of a given time (a period of one week was
approximated[31]) the lower chloroform containing
layer[32] was separated and analysis was performed
on it.

[22] More orotundity. (Rule 3)

[23] Warning Word. (Rule 3)

[24] This kind of shorthand "lab slang" seems very convenient to the speaker, but as with most alluring things, the price is high. Readers should never be subjected to it, for they cannot demand that the authors explain themselves. Listeners often misunderstand it, because the words have (for them) an obvious meaning which is *not* that intended. Lastly, the speaker may confuse himself through constant repetition of a phrase without considering its meaning. (Rule 2)

[25] Dangling participle. (Rule 2)

[26] Judgment: Know your audience. Readers of this paper can be expected to know what arterial adventitia is.

[27] All manipulations described in scientific papers are assumed to have been careful. (Rule 2)

[28] Noun cluster obscures meaning. (Rule 4)

[29] Grandilingua for "about." (Rule 1)

[30] Warning word ending in "ing." (Rule 2)

[31] Prime example of complickese. (Rule 1)

[32] That coffee containing cup again. (Rule 2)

aerobic extraction at much lower temperatures in
order to minimize oxidation.

MATERIALS AND METHODS

Aortic tissue[21]

Aortas were obtained at autopsy, within 6–12 hr
of death[22], at the University Hospital, Barchester.
Aortas were classified[23] as being at stage 0, I, II,
or III of atherosclerosis[24] according to the
appearance of the intima (6), and the adventitia
was rapidly removed.

Each preparation, comprising intima and media[25],
was immediately submerged[26] in about 100 volumes of
methanol–chloroform 2:1 (v/v)[27] and stored[28] at –20 °C.
After about one week the lower (lipid–containing)[29]
layer was separated and its peroxide content was
determined[30].

[21] Subheadings inserted as signposts.
[22] The shorthand jargon "6–12 hr autopsy" has been expanded to be comprehensible and precise. (Rule 2)
[23] Hidden verb "classify" released; colorless verb "done" eliminated. (Rule 3)
[24] Phrase condensed by elimination of unnecessary words. (Rule 1)
[25] More information given; also, more precise in making clear that the preparation consists of one piece of tissue (therefore singular verb).
[26] Diction: descriptive verb replaces colorless one.
[27] The "100 volumes" separated from "(v/v)" for clarity.
[28] Brevity achieved by release of hidden verb "store." (Rule 2)
[29] This clarifying adjective would not be necessary for the "in-group" but helps
a wider circle of readers without offending anyone.
[30] Abstract noun "analysis" replaced by precise phrase. (Rule 3)

In some cases[33] the aortic material was further extracted with the same solvent at room temperature with stirring, and subsequently at the reflux temperature. The further yield of lipid was never more than half that initially extracted; the peroxide value of this extract was negligible, thus proving[34] that extraction at the lower temperature did extract peroxides effectively.

To determine[35] the oxidizability of lipid while it[36] is still contained in the tissue, a few aorta preparations were halved and one part exposed[37] to the atmosphere at room temperature (25°C) for 30 minutes before extraction, while[38] the other was extracted immediately after removal of the adventitia.

Aliquots of the extracts were taken to dryness in tared glass shells for analysis[39] of total lipid content[39] and determination of peroxide contents were[40] conducted on similar aliquots.

---

[33] Warning word: "cases" (see Gowers, *Plain Words*). In medical work especially the word has special connotations and should be avoided where these are not desired. In more general usage ("in the case of sunflower seeds") it can often be omitted altogether. (Rule 1)

[34] Dangling participle.

[35] Dangling infinitive (rarer than dangling participle, but still common). Subject of the verb "determine" is the investigator, subject of the main clause is "aorta preparations."

[36] Antecedent ambiguous ("oxidizability"?). (Rule 2)

[37] Incorrect omission of the auxiliary. Verb needed, "was." Grammatically implied, "were." (Rule 2)

[38] Note correct usage of "while:" true simultaneity of action here. "Whereas" is preferable when contrast only is to be conveyed. (Rule 2)

[39] "Analysis" implies a fractionation, which is not employed here. Hence Rule 2 is violated.

[40] Incorrect number of the verb, because of "contamination" by the nearest noun. Always examine what is the subject of each verb. (Rule 2)

Some of the aortic material[31] was further extracted with the same solvent mixture[32] at room temperature with stirring, and subsequently under reflux[33]. The further yield of lipid never exceeded[34] one half of[35] that initially extracted; the lipid peroxide value of the second extract was negligible. These findings quashed the possibility that peroxides were not efficiently extracted at the lower temperature and permitted conclusions to be drawn from examination of the low-temperature extract exclusively[36].

To determine[37] how easily lipid is oxidized while it is still contained in the tissue, we divided a few aorta preparations into two. One part was exposed to the atmosphere at room temperature (25 °C)[38] for 30 minutes before extraction, while the other was extracted immediately after removal of the adventitia.

Total lipid concentration of each extract was determined by drying[39] a portion in a tared glass

[31] One way to eliminate "case."

[32] Slight increase in precision. (Rule 2)

[33] Slightly more concise. (Rule 1)

[34] Diction: a precise, meaningful verb has replaced three colorless words.

[35] *Expansion* for clarity!

[36] In order to express the train of thought fully, the writer has had to expand his statement. Conciseness is not invariably ideal.

Some results are mentioned in this Methods section. This is sometimes inevitable and should not be shunned if their inclusion clarifies procedure or experimental design. The reason for their appearance "out of order" should be made amply clear: another function of the phrase marked[36].

Furthermore, the method for determining peroxide value has not yet been described; if subheadings are used the reader will rapidly observe that this description is to be provided shortly.

[37] Infinitive no longer dangles.

[38] "at 25°C" would be briefer, but would jettison an important point, namely the implication that other investigators working at room temperature inadvertently allowed autoxidation to take place. On the other hand, room temperature must be specified because this varies from place to place.

[39] Dangling participle, of the least objectionable kind.

Iodimetric lipid peroxide determination[41] is conveniently precise, and accurate for samples containing more than 50 μeq of peroxides (7), but as generally applied it is too insensitive for aortic extracts[42]. The microiodimetric procedure of Proudie and Slope (8) is approximately 2 orders of magnitude[43] more sensitive than earlier methods and enabled[44] results to be obtained on extracts from single aortas. The procedure was as described (8)[45].

RESULTS

The results are shown in Table I. The number of values obtained for less diseased aortas is small, for the reasons given below. Examination of the table reveals that[46] the peroxide values obtained[47] are all very[48] much lower than those of Lufton and Sowerby (1), which ranged from 3, at their so-called[49] Stage I of atherosclerosis, to 17, at their Stage V, μeq/g lipid[50]. None[51] of our values exceeded 2 and most of them[52] were less than 1 μeq/g.

[41] Cluster; slight pause necessary to grasp meaning. (Rule 4)

[42] What differentiates aortic extracts from other extracts is not immediately clear.

[43] Grandiloquence, see Baker. (Rule 1)

[44] Although Webster now admits the usage in which "enable" is synonymous with "allow," it remains more elegant to enable only persons to do things, not to enable things to be done.

[45] The principle of a method should always be succinctly stated even though a reference to its extended description is given.

[46] All words before this point in this sentence are redundant. (Rule 1)

[47] Redundant. (Rule 1)

[48] This word is used oftener than is warranted in scientific literature. (Rule 1)

[49] This word has derogatory overtones and is best avoided.

[50] The clumsy word-order is not redeemed by a plethora of commas.

[51] The perspicacious reader will observe that if the values in Table I are correct, either this statement is wrong or the distribution of values was skew.

[52] Redundant. (Rule 1)

shell; the peroxide concentration of another·
portion was measured[40] by micro—iodimetry[41].

Determination of lipid peroxides by micro—iodimetry[42]

The iodimetric method for determination of lipid
peroxides is convenient, precise, and accurate for
samples containing more than 50 μeq of peroxides
(7), but as generally applied it is too insensitive
for use with extracts of single aortas[43], which
usually contain (especially if they are relatively
free from atherosclerotic lesions) a small total
amount of lipid which itself contains little
peroxide. The micro—iodimetric method of Proudie
and Slope (8) is about 100 times[44] as sensitive as
earlier methods and was successfully applied. It
employs electrometric titration of iodine liberated
from iodide by the peroxides in acid solution.

RESULTS

The results are shown in Tables I and II[45]. The
number of values obtained for less diseased aortas
is small, for the reasons given below. The peroxide
values in Table I are all much lower than those of
Lufton and Sowerby (1), which ranged from 3
("Stage I") to 17 ("Stage V") μeq/g lipid. Only
one of our values was higher than 2 and most were
below 1 μeq/g. There was no obvious correlation

---

[40] The hidden verb to be released was "determine" but because this has been used
earlier in the sentence, "measure" is substituted for variety.

[41] More information provided, and a link with the next section results.

[42] Subheading for guidance of the reader.

[43] Inclusion of an important point (single aorta) here clarifies the thought. There
is then no need to repeat the words later.

[44] A straightforward number is almost always to be preferred to "orders of
magnitude."

[45] The data have been separated into two tables because there were two points
to be made. See notes under the tables.

TABLE I

Peroxide values

Tissue exposed to air[a]			Tissue not exposed before extraction[a]		
Stage of athero-sclerosis	Tissue No.	Peroxide Content	Stage of athero-sclerosis	Tissue No.	Peroxide Content
		μeq/g			μeq/g
III[b]	21[c]	2.62	III[b]	1–13,20,21,22[c]	1.26 ± 0.91[d]
III[b]	22	1.64	II[b]	14–17	0.84 ± 0.30
I[b]	23	1.81	I[b]	18,23	1.18 ± 0.57[e]
			0[b]	19	0.41

General. Design of table is confused. One realizes this when he tries to expand the title to be informative: such a long title results that it is clear that two tables are needed, each to show a different point.

[a] Since one reads from left to right, it is normally better to show controls on the left.

[b] Similarly, as one reads downwards, it is usually best to show controls, or less-diseased samples, at the top.

[c] The numbers designating individual samples of aortic tissue are of no assistance to the reader unless he can compare values for any one tissue in different places in the table. Here individual values have, in the right-hand half of the table, been buried in means. No direct comparison is possible, as it is in Table II in the improved version.

[d] There is no indication whether this is Standard Deviation or Standard Error of the Mean. This must always be stated explicitly, together with the number of observations (readily deduced, in this case, from penultimate column).

[e] When there are only two values, it is simply foolish to report them thus.

Table I also shows that[53] when tissue was exposed to the air at 25 °C the peroxide value was increased 2–3 times (tissues 21–23), suggesting[25] very[48] strongly that in this situation[54] lipid peroxides are formed through an artifactual conversion[55] of the lipids before they are extracted. Since some exposure

[53] All words up to this point redundant. (Rule 1)

[54] Warning word: often indicates that the writer is not thinking. Here the phrase can be deleted altogether.

[55] Circumlocution.

TABLE I

Peroxide values of lipids from aortas at different
stages of atherosclerosis

Stage of Atherosclerosis	No. of aortas	Peroxide Content
		μeq/g
0	1	0.41
I	2	0.61, 1.75
II	4	0.84 ± 0.30*
III	16	1.26 ± 0.91*

* Standard Deviation

TABLE II

Effect on lipid peroxide levels of exposing tissue
to air before extraction of the lipids

Aorta No.	Stage of Atherosclerosis	Peroxide Content	
		Extracted immediately	Exposed*
		μeq/g	μeq/g
1	I	0.61	1.81
2	III	0.81	1.64
3	III	0.80	2.62

* For 30 min at 25 °C

General. The titles and layout expose experimental design completely to a reader who has not yet looked at the text; this reader is also given crucial information succinctly in the footnote to Table II.

between peroxide content and stage of atherosclerosis[46].

Exposure of the tissue to air at room temperature
increased the peroxide value 2–3 times (Table II),
which strongly suggests[47] that lipid peroxides are
easily formed artifactually[48] before the lipids can

---

[46] An extra, important conclusion has been added.
[47] Replaces dangling participle.
[48] Replaces circumlocutory phrase.

cannot be avoided during manipulation[56] at autopsy
and during removal of adventitia, all values in
Table I are likely[57] too high. Based on[58] this
result, and coupled with the fact that even these
sensitive methods do not have the ability to yield
an accurate result on the small amounts of lipid
obtainable from Stage 0 or I aortas, the project
of comparing peroxide contents of aortas with
varying[59] degrees of atherosclerosis has been
abandoned at the present time[60].

DISCUSSION

If, as seems likely from these results, the high
values of Lufton and Sowerby (1) for the aorta
lipid peroxide content[61] were due to artifactual
formation of peroxides [during tissue preparation
and possibly during the extraction of the lipids]*,
[the question arises]*, why did these authors
obtain a correlation of peroxide content with
atherosclerosis? [At the time of their investigation
(1951) it was not known that]* the arterial lipid
unsaturation index[61] increases with increasing
degree of atherosclerosis. This increasing
unsaturation, most striking in the cholesteryl
esters, was shown by Gee et al. (6) [with the aid
of gas—liquid chromatography]*. Furthermore, the

---

[56] Redundant polysyllable. (Rule 1)
[57] Adjective, now accepted by Webster as adverb, still grates on some people in this usage.
[58] Beware: this phrase is often discovered to harbor a dangling past participle, as here. (Rule 2)
[59] Frequently, and shamefully, misused. "Varying" is a continuous process and the word should not be confused with "various" or "different." (Rule 2)
[60] Redundant. (Rule 1)
[61] Noun cluster. (Rule 4)
* There are few stylistic or grammatical errors in the Discussion; it is made too long not by roundabout phraseology but by the inclusion of irrelevancies, marked [ ]*.

be extracted. Since some exposure is inevitable
during autopsy and removal of adventitia, all
values in Table I are likely to be[49] too high. For
this reason, and because even these sensitive
methods are incapable[50] of giving an accurate result
on the small amounts of lipid that can be extracted[51]
from Stage 0 or I aortas, the project of comparing
peroxide contents of aortas with differing[52] degrees
of atherosclerosis has been abandoned.

DISCUSSION[53]

If the peroxides measured in lipid extracts from
the arterial wall are artifacts, how can we
explain Lufton and Sowerby's findings (1) that
the peroxide content is correlated with degree of
atherosclerosis? It has recently been discovered
(6) that arterial lipids become progressively more
unsaturated with increasing degree of atherosclerosis. Among the lipid classes, cholesteryl
esters show the most striking increase in
unsaturation, and the proportion of cholesteryl
esters relative to the other lipids also rises
(9, 10). The more atherosclerotic the aorta,
therefore, the more susceptible will its lipids be

---

[49] Note insertion. The correction can sometimes be made by substituting "probably" for "likely."

[50] Replaces roundabout phrase.

[51] Substituted for "obtainable" for variety: "incapable . . . obtainable" had an
ugly jingle (fine point, can be omitted).

[52] Another way of correcting "varying."

[53] The argument here is tighter because the writer has eliminated irrelevant
information and has worked on his connectives.

proportion of cholesteryl esters relative to the
other lipids rises also, [as has long been recog-
nized]* (9, 10). The atherosclerotic aorta therefore
bears an increasingly oxidizable lipid load, and
this would be sufficiently explanatory[62] of the
results obtained.

We should like[63] to point out, however, that
lipid peroxidation may still be involved somehow
in the inception of atherosclerosis or in forwarding
its progress. Although only small amounts of lipid
peroxides were found, they[64] might be genuine
components of the tissue. The possibility also
exists that more were present in the living patient,
but decomposed between the time of death and the
autopsy. Their very decomposition in the living
tissue might have been the cause of atherosclerotic
changes. But it is not our opinion[65] that measurement
of peroxides in necropsy material can elucidate
this problem[66].

REFERENCES

1. L. Lufton[a] and J. Sowerby. 1952. <u>Acta pathol.
   et.</u>[b] <u>microbiology</u>[c] 30:492.

---

[62] Verb here is hidden in an adjective for a change; the resultant construction is
no less stilted.

[63] This kind of absurd conditional should be avoided: the authors *are* pointing
it out. (Rule 2)

[64] Is antecedent "amounts" or "peroxides"? (Rule 2)

[65] Circumlocution. (Rule 1)

[66] Warning word: note again how it enables an author to be vague. What, of the
several speculative statements in preceding sentences, does the author regard
as "the problem?"

If you wish, you can use the editing assignment to provide instruction on giving
references correctly, in a consistent style. The basis for analyzing these muddled
references is the "correct form" given on the opposite page, in the Improved
Text. The deviations above are as follows:

[a] Initial precedes surname of first author.

[b] Period placed after a word that is not an abbreviation.

[c] Written out in full, incorrectly (obvious from the rest that journal title is in
Latin).

to oxidation during dissection; this effectively explains the observed correlation.

Our results do not exclude the possibility that lipid peroxides play a role in atherogenesis or in the development of atherosclerosis. The small amounts found may not be entirely artifactual. Furthermore, lipid peroxides present in vivo may decompose between death and autopsy. More importantly, they may have formed earlier in the patient's life and subsequently decomposed, with the undesirable consequences mentioned in the Introduction. We do not believe, however, that their possible role in atherosclerosis has been or can be established by examination of the lipids after death.

REFERENCES

1. Lufton, L., and J. Sowerby. 1952. Acta Pathol. Microbiol. 30: 492.

2. Robarts, M., D. O. Omnium[d] and G. Dumbello,[d]
   1961. J. Perfect Res.[d] 2:631.
3. Neroni, M. V. 1953. Bull. Soc. ital. sper.
   Biol.[e] 92:16.
4. De Courcy, E. 1963. Extrait de[f] Bull. Soc.
   Chem.[g] France 116:214.
5. Hartletop, M. O. J. Gerontol.[h] 63, 321 (1958)[i].
6. Gee, N. B., Whiz, A. C.[j] and W. A. Goof[k] Scalpel
   i:137[m], 1960.
7. Eaxes, J. and Buffle, R. (ed.) Organic Peroxide
   Analysis 1:376, 1856[n].
8. Proudie, M. B., and O. Slope. (1964). J. W.
   M.[p] 3:423.
9. Dunstable, E., et al.[q] Biochem.[g] Biophys. Acta
   74:111, 1957.
10. Doppelganger,[r] D., and D. Winterreise. Z. Phys.[s]
    Chem. 216 (1915) 984.

[d] Comma omitted; comma substituted for period after "Dumbello"; underscoring omitted.
[e] Arbitrary decisions on capitalization of each abbreviation.
[f] Blind copying from the heading on the reprint.
[g] Misspelled foreign word that is similar to English equivalent.
[h] Underscoring omitted.
[i] Incorrect form for volume, page, year.
[j] Initials should precede name of second author.
[k] Period omitted.
[m] Last digit of page number dropped.
[n] A multitude of faults, including misspelling of author's name, grossly wrong
date, the treatment of a book as a journal, and the omission of the publisher
and place of publication.
[p] Unpardonable to refer to a journal by initials only.
[q] All authors must be given.
[r] Foreigners like to receive all their diacritical marks.
[s] Complete confusion possible as a result of wrong abbreviation.

2. Robarts, M., D. O. Omnium, and G. Dumbello. 1961. J. Perfect Res. 2: 631.
3. Neroni, M. V. 1953. Bull. Soc. Ital. Sper. Biol. 92: 16.
4. De Courcy, E. 1963. Bull. Soc. Chim. Fr. 116: 214.
5. Hartletop, M. O. 1958. J. Gerontol. 63: 321.
6. Gee, N. B., A. C. Whiz, and W. A. Goof. 1960. Scalpel. i: 1378.
7. Eames, J. 1956. In Organic Peroxide Analysis. Sir Raffle Buffle, editor. Cathedral Publishers, Barchester. 1: 376.
8. Proudie, M. B., and O. Slope. 1964. J. Workable Methods. 3: 423.
9. Dunstable, E., F. Gresham, and M. Thorne. 1957. Biochim. Biophys. Acta. 74: 111.
10. Doppelgänger, D., and D. Winterreise. 1915. Hoppe-Seyler's Z. Physiol. Chem. 216: 984.

References. Note consistency of styling. This is, unfortunately, different for each journal; the style of the chosen journal must be rigorously followed. For abbreviation of journal titles, see p. 26, second paragraph.

Reconsideration of Title
Now that you have read the paper, do you think any of the following titles is better than the one suggested?

1. Evidence that Lipid Peroxides Detected in Extracts of Human Aorta Are Artifacts.
2. Lipid Peroxides Found in Human Aorta Lipids Are Artifacts.
3. Are Lipid Peroxides in Extracts of Human Aorta Artifacts?
4. Artifactual Formation of Peroxides in Lipids Extracted from Human Aorta.
5. Peroxide Formation in Lipids of Human Aorta.
6. Peroxide Formation in Lipids Extracted from Human Aorta.

ASSIGNMENT 2: FAULTY TEXT

AN EXAMINATION OF THE MEASURES TAKEN BY PHYSICAL FITNESS TESTS AND THEIR INFLUENCE ON FINAL TEST SCORES

Woody Lissen and Way Behind

INTRODUCTION

Cardiovascular-function and general bodily efficiency relationships[1] have formed the subject of a great deal of research[2] in order to gauge[3] the general health of individuals. Workers in the physical fitness field have often been puzzled by the lack of agreement in results shown by tests all purporting to measure this[4] general trait.

This study attempted to separate the similarities and dissimilarities[5] underlying measurements which were[6] derived from several such tests, all of[6] which have found support in one or more of the services. The tests in question[6] were the Behnke step-up test (1), the Harvard step-up test (2), and the Schneider index of physical fitness (3).

General note. This is a much shorter example than the preceding one and is not intended to be criticized for lack of data or documentation for the conclusions. No tables are provided.

Title. Too general, and unnecessarily wordy. If the type of examination were precisely specified, the phrase "their influence in final test scores" could be eliminated.

[1] Impressive noun cluster. (Rule 4)

[2] The alert reviser will detect wordiness by noticing the number of words without much content: "formed," "subject," "great deal."

[3] Dangling infinitive, not disguised by "in order."

[4] Antecedent unclear.

[5] One word (e.g., disparity) is better. (Rule 1)

[6] Awkward and unnecessary. Why not simply "measurements derived?" The addition of such unnecessary material makes for a turgid and dreary style. (Rule 1)

ASSIGNMENT 2: IMPROVED TEXT

STATISTICAL EVALUATION OF THREE[1]
TESTS OF PHYSICAL FITNESS[2]
UTILIZED BY THE ARMED FORCES

Heed More and H. E. Ketchup

INTRODUCTION

Physical fitness tests rely on the relationship between cardiovascular function and bodily efficiency to provide an index of general health. Students of human physiology are disturbed by the poor correlations among tests that are supposed to measure a single characteristic, physical fitness. The study summarized here[3] attempts to explain the disparity among three fitness tests currently utilized in the Armed Forces: the Behnke step-up test (1), the Harvard step-up test (2), and the Schneider index of physical fitness (3).

[1] Since there are many tests of physical fitness in use, the title should indicate the study's limitations.

[2] The title could end here, but the additional information furnished by the third line indicates the relevance of the study and narrows its application—for instance, the Director of Activities at Leisure World need not have a copy in his library!

[3] Let the reader know at the onset that the paper is a summary so that he will not expect a great deal of detail. (Consideration for audience)

THE TESTS[7]

The 120 randomly selected subjects were chosen by separating from a main group of approximately 400 men (enlisted candidates for submarine training) the occupants of chairs which had been previously secretly marked. Strict control[8] of the lives of the subjects was maintained[9] by regulating[10] their activities during an experimental period which lasted for three days. They were quartered in a special barracks and ate at a separate mess.

Correlation[11] exhibited by the tests utilized in this study[12] was found to be poor. The endurance phase of the Behnke test had a correlation of 0.231 with the Harvard test and 0.038 with the Schneider index. The two latter tests had correlations of 0.282 and 0.284 for the cardiovascular phase of the Behnke test[13,14]. Thus, this particular study[12] gives support to claims of other studies (4,5) that various tests all of which[12] claim to measure the general trait of physical fitness show a poor correlation.

To explain[15] this noticeable lack of correlation, it was decided that the data would be appraised further by means of the Adjutant General's Office (Army) – modified Thurstone Group Centroid method[1].

---

[7] Too vague to serve as a guide to the reader and incorrect to boot. The section doesn't describe the tests themselves but rather the general procedure. (Rule 2)

[8] What aspects of the subjects' lives were "strictly controlled"? (Rule 2)

[9] Warning word. Verb needed: "controlled" or "regulated." (Rule 3)

[10] Dangling participle

[11] Too vague. Correlation with what? (Rule 2)

[12] Unnecessary; simply adds to wordiness. (Rule 1)

[13] Don't switch order of comparison; this makes it harder for reader to follow.

[14] A general statement of the low correlation is sufficient in a summary. Incidentally, nowhere in this text is the reader informed that the paper is merely a summary.

[15] Dangling infinitive.

PROCEDURE

The sample of 120 men was randomly selected from 400 enlisted candidates processed through the Submarine Training School[4]. The fitness tests were part of a battery of measures being considered for their possible value in selecting men for submarine duty[5]. The tests were administered in random order, one on each afternoon of a 3–day experimental period during which the daily program and diets of the subjects were strictly regulated.

STATISTICAL ANALYSIS[6]

Correlation coefficients were determined for 35 variables (see Table 1)* selected from the test measures. The poor correlation exhibited between the final scores of the three tests (0.282 for Behnke and Harvard, 0.284 for Behnke and Schneider, 0.082 for Harvard and Schneider) was in keeping with the results of other studies (4,5).

The data were further examined by a modified (6) Thurstone group centroid method (7) of factor

---

[4] Sufficient to give the idea that the total group was large enough for the 120 subjects to be representative; unnecessary methodological detail eliminated.

[5] This will tell the reader why the tests were considered important enough to proceed with an involved analysis when initial results were not encouraging.

[6] Another heading here helps the reader.

* See footnote on p. 78; the tables in this example are imaginary.

Results of the factorial appraisal of physical
fitness data[16] will be discussed in as general terms
as possible[17] for the benefit of the nonstatistical
reader.

RESULTS AND DISCUSSION

If occasionally this general discussion of statistical results gives rise to the impression that
some of the utterances are "ex cathedra"[18], it is
emphasized that there is a statistical justification
for all conclusions drawn, as indicated by
available verifications presented in the table of
intercorrelations, the table of factor loadings,
and the table of residuals[19].

This paper does not attempt to delineate the
physiological functions which should be included
in an estimate of the general trait of physical
fitness and thus infringe on the rights of
specialists in the area of physical fitness[20].
There is no implication intended that the functions
isolated by this study are the only valuable components in gauging physical fitness but rather
that they are the only physiological functions
actually measured by the tests investigated[21]. When
there has been[22] substantial agreement among

[16] Long, unnecessary, and repetitious. (Rule 1)
[17] Why not simply "in general terms"? (Rule 1)
[18] Pompous. The second part of the sentence documents the findings. In general,
Latin phrases (including *vide supra* and *circa*) should be regarded as "warning
words" and translated.
[19] Why not simply refer to the tables by number? If the reader is not statistically
oriented, such words as factor loadings and residuals won't mean anything.
(Rule 1)
[20] First, let's tell the reader what the analysis shows. This section is really *Discussion* not *Results*. In any case, it contains unnecessary verbiage.
[21] Faulty parallelism garbles the thought. Make into two sentences. (Rule 1)
[22] "There has been," "there is" often indicate that a passive voice is longing to
be made active.

analysis, which attempts to explain the correlation coefficients in terms of a number of factors or underlying bases of association[7].

RESULTS AND RECOMMENDATIONS

Results will be presented in general terms for the convenience of readers who are not statistically oriented. Statistical verification of the statements can be found in Tables 2 and 3.

---

[7] Even the nonstatistical reader will want to know that correlation coefficients are the "raw data" for factor analysis.

specialists on just what components of physical
fitness should be represented in a physical
fitness[23] appraisal and just[24] how important each
component is relative[24] to such an estimate, test
scores may then be devised accordingly[24] to
represent these factors according to their appropriate percentages. The present study offers a
way in which an evaluation may be made to sys-
tematize fitness estimates for it has shown that
the tests investigated indicate that the influence
of physiological functions is a reflection of the
scoring method involved.

The following conclusions are drawn from the
findings of the present study[25]:

1. A basic resting pulse rate tends to characterize
each individual, tends to remain relatively constant
during any given day, appears to have[26] low day-to-
day reliability, and does not warrant making
predictions as to the results of readings taken on
the next or any other day[27].

2. Pulse response to prolonged violent exercise is
a basic physiological factor[28] and meaningful[29]
classification of individuals may be made[30] on the
basis of this factor.

3. Endurance time in seconds is a component[31] which
is a basic repeatable measure of individual
differences. Items contributing to the lowering
of endurance scores for a given individual are

---

[23] Repetitious.

[24] Examination of the meaning of these words reveals them to be redundant.

[25] Unnecessary verbiage. From what other study would they be drawn? (Rule 1)

[26] Excess of caution. (Rule 2)

[27] "low day-to-day reliability" is sufficient for the reader to draw a conclusion;
rest of sentence unnecessary. Rule 2 might expose the fault, Rule 1 dictates
deletion.

[28] What use do the test scores make of this factor? (Purpose of article forgotten)

[29] An overworked word. (Rule 2)

[30] Warning of a hidden verb. (Rule 3)

[31] Component of what? (Rule 2)

The principal findings were as follows:

1. A basic resting pulse rate characterizes each individual and tends to remain constant during any given day. However, day-to-day stability is low. If this measure is employed to estimate an individual's fitness for a particular task, it should be determined on the day of the assignment itself[8].

2. Pulse response to prolonged violent exercise is a basic physiological factor upon which a useful classification of individuals may be based. Unfortunately, scoring methods give little weight to this factor.

3. Endurance time in seconds is a basic repeatable measure of an individual's physical fitness. Items that contribute to the lowering of the endurance score include[9] (a) high increase in pulse rate

---

[8] Makes conclusion significant in terms of the purpose of the study.

[9] Word "include" is better than the "are" used on page 84. The implication is that still other factors may also be contributing. (Rule 2)

high increase in pulse rate following violent
exercise, slow return of pulse rate to normal after
exercise, high standing[32] in size–strength variables[32],
and increasing age.
4. A basic resting blood pressure level[33] is
characteristic of each individual and considerably[34]
influences his pulse reactions to exercise. This[35]
is also true of variability in blood pressure level
attributed to slight changes in environmental
conditions.
5. The advantage of the classification potential[36]
present in the measures taken and then not utilized
is not reflected in the final test scores for the
three tests.

[32] Meaning? Jargon like this should be eliminated by Step 24.
[33] Stacked modifiers. (Rule 4)
[34] Omit this "hedging" word; it belongs to a class of vague qualifiers of dubious
    utility.
[35] Antecedent unclear. (Rule 2)
[36] This vogue-word is always suspect.

after violent exercise, (b) slow return of pulse
rate to normal after exercise, (c) high values in
measurements of the subject's size compared to his
strength, and (d) increasing age. We recommend that
upper age ceilings be established for any Armed
Services task that requires long maintenance of
violent bodily activity[8].
4. Each person has a characteristic blood pressure
level at rest and the reaction of his pulse rate to
exercise is related to this resting level. Variation
in level with slight changes in environmental
conditions is also characteristic of the individual.
Two of the tests investigated do not include
such measures; the other does include several
measures of blood pressure but virtually ignores
them in the scoring formula.
5. The fitness tests vary widely in the choice of
physiological functions which they actually measure
and in the contributions of these items to final
test scores.

DISCUSSION

Delineation of the physiological functions which
should be included in an estimate of the general
trait of "physical fitness" is outside our province.
We do not mean to imply that the functions isolated
by the factor analysis described are the only
components of value in gauging physical fitness.
The point is rather that they are the only physiological functions actually measured by the tests
named.

The results clearly indicate that the tests
employed at present should be reevaluated and
systematized. For example, a certain pulse reaction
to prolonged violent exercise has been shown to be
characteristic of the individual. One of the tests

ASSIGNMENT 3: FAULTY TEXT

SOME STUDIES[1] ON A RAPID BIOASSAY MICROMETHOD[2]
A. Clodd
INTRODUCTION

Many authors, including[3] this laboratory (3)[4], have been engaged in the study of the identification[5] and detection[5] of specific[6] biologically active mole-

This editing assignment was kindly provided by Dr. William R. Lockhart, Department of Bacteriology, Iowa State University.

[1] See Step 22 (p. 104) on the need to avoid unnecessary words like these.

[2] Too vague. Students should read the whole article, then apply Rule 2 (Make Sure of the Meaning of Every Word) in making the title more precise.

[3] Can authors include a laboratory? (Rule 2)

[4] In this Assignment, a method of numbering references different from that in Assignment 1 is exemplified. The references here have been arranged alphabetically according to the first author's name and then numbered consecutively, instead of being numbered in the order of their appearance in the text. Both systems for citing references are actually used. What are the advantages of each?

[5] Abstract nouns derived from verbs. First target for revision! (Rule 3, Use Verbs Instead of Abstract Nouns)

[6] Overworked word, which has a definite and useful meaning, but which is often inserted to stop a gap in the author's thoughts.

[DISCUSSION–continued]

contains no estimate of this function, and the other two give little weight to it in their scoring methods. Moreover, resting blood pressure and variability in blood pressure are both components that can form the basis for useful classification, but two of the tests exclude these measures and the third virtually ignores their influence in the final test score.

When specialists in physical fitness agree on just what components should be represented and assess their relative importance, test scores may be devised to incorporate these factors in the appropriate percentages[10].

[10] Indicates the definitive action required and places the statement in a prominent place—the end.

ASSIGNMENT 3: IMPROVED TEXT

RAPID MICROMETHOD FOR DETECTION AND IDENTIFICATION OF AMINO ACIDS WITH AUXOTROPHIC BACTERIA[1]

S. Briter

INTRODUCTION

Many[2] authors (2–4) have used autographic methods to detect and identify biologically required molecules (for review see ref. 4). In the auto–

[1] Title is longer, but much more informative. "Bioassay" has been replaced by the actual kinds of assay meant (detection and identification). The kind of molecules assayed (amino acids) is specified. (Although the method may be applicable to other kinds of molecules, this paper deals only with amino acids.) Finally, the *kind* of method (namely, a bacteriological one) is indicated and the intelligent reader immediately recognizes the principle on which it is based (auxotrophic bacteria are mutant bacteria with specific nutrient requirements).

[2] If there are many authors, give them—or examples of them—not just your own name or that of colleagues!

cules by autographic methods. This problem[7] has recently been reviewed (4). These[8] procedures, in which
nutritionally deficient mutant bacteria are suspended in minimal media and show zones of growth
following[9] incubation in the presence of the required nutrilite, are in possession of a multi-
plicity[10] of advantages over the more[11] conventional
bioassay techniques being conducted in liquid media.
These[12] include not only simplicity[13] of technique but
also involve[14] the reduction[5] of interference[5] from
inhibitory materials which may reveal their presence[13] in crude sample extracts as natural constituents, or as inadvertent extraction procedure residues[15] (5), as well as their[16] direct applicability[5]
to paper chromatograms where they may aid in the
identification[5] of spots[17]. Their principal disadvantage, being[18] that samples of relatively[19] high
concentration are required, has been largely com-
pensated for by the incorporation[5] of tetrazolium
salts in the solid[20] bioassay medium. Reduction[5] of
these compounds occurs[14] during growth[5] of the test

[7] What problem? (Rule 2)

[8] Warning word. In this case the author passes the test: antecedent ("autographic
methods") is unambiguous and reasonably close by.

[9] Warning word—ends in "ing." *After* always preferable as a preposition.

[10] Grandiloquence. (Rule 1, Be Simple and Concise)

[11] Necessary? (Rule 2)

[12] Antecedent "techniques" or "advantages"? (Rule 2)

[13] Abstract noun derived from adjective. Be simple. (Rule 1)

[14] Warning word—colorless verb, which can probably be replaced by a vigorous
one. See Table 1 of Chapter 6

[15] String of modifiers (Rule 4, Break Up Noun Clusters and Stacked Modifiers).
As so frequently happens, unraveling the string shows how inappropriate some
of the adjectives are.

[16] Antecedent "residues", "materials"? (Rule 2)

[17] The polysyllabic fog has swallowed up all meaning by this time.

[18] Awkward construction.

[19] Relative to what? (Warning word; Rule 2)

[20] The first we are told about this. Anyway, agar is *not* solid.

graphic procedure, nutritionally deficient mutant
bacteria with specific nutrient requirements are
suspended in an agar medium in a petri dish or on a
glass plate.[3] After incubation with the required
nutrilite they show zones of growth.

The technique has many advantages over conventional bioassays in liquid media. It[4] is simpler;
it is not subject to interference by inhibitors that
occur naturally in crude sample extracts or result
from extraction procedures (3); and it can be used
directly to identify the small amounts of material
contained in spots cut out from paper chromatograms.[5] The main disadvantage, namely that
concentrated samples are required, has been overcome
in one laboratory (3) by the incorporation of
tetrazolium salts in the agar medium. These salts

[3] Specific details are given, to bring the technique vividly before the reader's
eye. These details can all be deduced by your students from later passages in
the Faulty Text.

[4] Warning word, but the antecedent ("technique") is in fact unambiguous. In the
sentence that follows, the expressions have been simplified by the substitution
of verbs for abstract nouns. In addition, the ideas are conveyed in three parallel
sentences. Parallel constructions are easy for the reader to follow, especially
when the writer is giving a list, as here.

[5] Expansion for clarity. The technique was *not* "applied directly to paper
chromatograms," but to spots cut out from paper chromatograms.

bacteria, giving criteria of response[5] the sensitivity of which is greater than with tube assay
(4,5). A method here presented holds promise[5] of
offering a further increase in sensitivity[13] and
economy of time, which may possibly further enhance
the potential[21] usefulness[13] of bioautography methods.

METHODS

The test organism used was a series of auxotrophic
mutants of E. coli, and a strain of Lactobacillus
arabinosus. The organism was first grown in nutrient
broth and cells from log phase cultures[22]
centrifuged[23], followed[24] by washing, and a resuspen-
sion[5] then[23] made[14] in 2X minimal medium. The R medium
(1) was employed[25] for E. coli and pantothenate assay
medium, on the other hand, was used in experiments
involving L. arabinosus. The cell suspension is[26] now
mixed with equal volumes of 3% agar, liquefied and
cooled[27] to 45 °C. Adjustment[5] of the suspension is
undertaken[14] so that the density of the seeded agar
approximated 10^5 or 10^6 cells per ml.

   The sample of the growth factor being assayed
need not always be the same,[28] in some cases it was a
small section cut from a paper chromatogram, but
in these[29] experiments designed to calibrate the
method it[29] consisted of measured quantities (up to
0.1 ml) of a solution of the growth factor being

---

[21] "Possibly . . . potential" is redundant and pompous. (Rule 1)

[22] The sort of noun cluster that close examination shows to be inaccurate.

[23] Omitted auxiliary.

[24] Warning word ending in "ed" (especially ambiguous in this context because
it is preceded by a genuine past participle).

[25] Bombastic variant of "used"; pointless variation of verb within the sentence.
(Rule 1)

[26] Mixed tenses (see footnote 10, Improved Text).

[27] Ambiguity: was the *mixture* liquefied and cooled, or only the agar?

[28] Incorrect punctuation.

[29] Antecedent?

are reduced if the test bacteria grow, and the resultant blue color can be detected with a sensitivity greater than in the tube assay.

The technique presented here further increases the sensitivity of the method and makes it less time-consuming.[6]

METHODS

The organisms used were a strain of Lactobacillus arabinosus and a series of auxotrophic mutants of Escherichia coli.[7] Each organism was grown in nutrient broth and cells in log-phase growth were centrifuged, washed, and resuspended in double-strength[8] minimal medium. For E. coli, R medium (1) was used; for L. arabinosus, pantothenate assay medium.[9] The cell suspension was[10] mixed with an equal volume of 3% aqueous agar that had been liquefied and cooled to 45 °C. The suspension was diluted until it contained[11] 10^5-10^6 cells per ml.

The sample of amino acid or other growth factor being assayed need not always be in solution (for example, it may be in the form of a spot cut from a paper chromatogram), but in the calibrating experiments it consisted of measured quantities (up to 0.1 ml) of an aqueous solution. The sample was placed in

---

[6] Note division of the Introduction into three paragraphs: (a) general orientation and description of autography; (b) advantages and disadvantages of the method to date; (c) advantages of technique to be described.

[7] Consistency. If *Lactobacillus* is spelled out (as it should be, when first mentioned), *Escherichia* must be, too.

[8] "Double strength" has replaced the laboratory jargon "2 ×."

[9] Notice the conciseness of parallel constructions.

[10] In descriptions of a method recommended for future use, the present tense may be used and is appropriate if a final "recipe" is being presented. However, the writer must avoid mixing past and present, and when he is describing not only the method but also tests of the method (for which the past tense would be needed) it is best to stick to the past.

[11] Removal of the verb "approximated" and use of Rule 2 showed that "density" was entirely misused.

analyzed[30]. The sample, whether a drop of a solution,
or a section of paper, or a sample of varying[31]
nature[32], is then placed in the center of a sterile
microscope slide, presterilized[33] in petri dishes,
and the inoculum of[10] one drop of seeded agar added.
If a liquid sample volume[34] is large, it should be
permitted to evaporate first.[35] A warmed, sterile
coverslip is then placed immediately over the agar,
which flows to the edges of the cover slip and
solidifies almost at once. In order to assure[36]
spreading of the agar in a thin, uniform layer,
prewarming[33] of the slides by incubation or by some
other means[10] would appear[37] to be indicated[14]. Due
to[38] the tendency of evaporation[5] of agar during subsequent incubation[5], the edges of the coverslip may
be sealed to the slide with paraffin, and[39] the
slides were[26] incubated at 37°C. Growth response[5] may
be ascertained within a few hours, however[40] slides
sealed in this[29] manner may be stored without more
than minimal[41] drying of the agar for several days
or even weeks after preparation[5], if the investigator so desires.[42]

RESULTS

Response[5] to relatively[19] large concentrations of
sample is detectable upon gross macroscopic examina-

[30] Meaning of this word? (Rule 2)
[31] Forbid this word except when *continuous* variation is meant.
[32] Woolly word, see Table 1 of Chapter 6 and Gowers.
[33] The fatuous "pre." (Rule 1)
[34] Noun cluster. (Rule 4)
[35] Illogical order of description.
[36] Dangling infinitive. (Rule 2)
[37] Outlaw "would appear" under all circumstances. (Rule 1)
[38] Warning word: "because of" almost always better.
[39] Inappropriate conjunction.
[40] Common misuse for "but." (Rule 1)
[41] Warning word, see Table 1 of Chapter 6.
[42] Pompous verbal flourish. (Rule 1)